soho theatre

Soho Theatre present

The Christ of Coldharbour Lane

by Oladipo Agboluaje

First performed at Soho Theatre on 31 May 2007

Soho Theatre is supported by

  Bloomberg

  Harold Hyam Wingate Foundation

Oladipo Agboluaje is Soho Theatre's Pearson Playwright in residence.

Performances in the Lorenz Auditorium
Registered Charity No: 267234

Soho Theatre present

The Christ of Coldharbour Lane

by Oladipo Agboluaje

Omotunde (Omo)	**Jimmy Akingbola**
Sarah Green	**Kay Bridgeman**
Maria Maudlin	**Dona Croll**
Dona	**Nadine Marshall**
Robbie Wedderburn	**Mark Monero**
Greg / Kingston / Jason	**Javone Prince**

All other characters played by members of the cast

Director	**Paulette Randall**
Designer	**Libby Watson**
Lighting Designer	**John Bishop**
Sound Designer	**Dan Steele**
Costume Designer	**Susannah Henry**
Choreographer	**David Leighton**
Fight Director	**Terry King**
Assistant Director	**Antoinette Lester**
Casting	**Nadine Hoare**

Production Manager	**Matt Noddings**
Stage Manager	**Dani Youngman**
Deputy Stage Manager	**Joanne Grabham**
Assistant Stage Manager	**Natasha Emma Jones**
Wardrobe Supervisor	**Sydney Florence**

Head Technician	**Nick Blount**
Head of Lighting	**Christoph Wagner**
Technician	**Mark Watts**

Scenery built and painted by **Scena Projects Ltd.**

Oladipo Agboluaje would like to thank: Lisa Goldman, Nina Steiger, Nadine Hoare, the management and staff of Soho Theatre, Paulette and the company, Gabriel Gbadamo, Nick Oshikanlu and Anthony Davies.

Press Representation: Nancy Poole (020 7478 0142)

Soho Theatre, 21 Dean Street, London W1D 3NE
Admin: 020 7287 5060 Fax: 020 7287 5061 Box Office: 0870 429 6883
www.sohotheatre.com

Writer

Oladipo Agboluaje *Writer*

Oladipo Agboluaje is Soho Theatre's Pearson Playwright in residence. *The Estate*, a co-production between Soho Theatre and Tiata Fahodzi, was produced last year. Other plays include: *Early Morning* (Oval House); *Mother Courage and her Children* (Eclipse Theatre); *For One Night Only* (PBAB); *British-ish* (New Wolsey Youth Theatre); *Captain Britain* (Talawa), *God is a DJ* (Theatre Centre). Works in progress include commissions for the National Theatre Studio and New Wolsey Theatre, Ipswich.

Cast

Jimmy Akingbola
Omotunde (Omo)

Theatre credits include: *Henry VIII* (RSC/AandBC); *The Cut* (Donmar Warehouse); *After the End* (Paines Plough); *The Estate* (Cheltenham Literary Festival); *White Open Spaces*, *3 Days in July*, *Playing Fields* (Soho Theatre); *Prayer Room* (Birmingham Rep/Edinburgh Lyceum); *Blue/Orange* (Winner 2005 TMA Best Supporting Actor Award – Sheffield Crucible); *People Next Door* (Edinburgh Traverse/Stratford East); *Thumbelina* (Stephen Joseph Theatre); *Naked Justice* (West Yorkshire Playhouse/Tour); *Baby Doll* (National Theatre/Albery); *The Changeling* (National Theatre); *Nativity*, *The Shooky*, *Behzti* (Birmingham Rep); *Ramayana* (National Theatre/Birmingham Rep);

Ready or Not (Stratford East). Television credits include: *Holby Blue*; *Longford*; *Blackbeard*; *Holby City*; *Doctors*; *The Crouches*; *Stupid*; *Roger Roger*; *The Bill*; *The Royal*; *Who Killed PC Blakelock*; *The Slightly Filthy Show*. Film credits include: *The Car; Anansi; The Dimples Cry*. Radio includes: *Eat Your Heart Out; Just Like Ronaldinho; Objects of Insane Desire; Ibadan; Troilus and Cressida; The Fire Children; A Noise in the Night; Clothes of Nakedness; Westway; Trinidad Sisters; Dancing Backwards*.

Kay Bridgeman *Sarah Green / Citizen / Woman 2 / Woman / Punter 2 / Passenger*

Theatre credits include: *Ma Rainey's Black Bottom* (Royal Exchange); *Shiver* – Silver Tongue Theatre Company (Pleasance); *Little Sweet Thing* Eclipse Theatre Company (Hampstead Theatre); *Car Thieves* (Birmingham Rep); *Sing Yer Heart Out for the Lads* (RNT); *Exclude Me* (Chelsea); *King Lear*, *Mules* (Contact); *Talking in Tongues* (Crucible). Television credits include: *Doctors*; *Rocket Man*; *Holby City*; *Red Cap*; *The Eustace Brothers*; *Murder In Mind*; *Cutting It*; *The Bill*; *Bhangra Heads*; *Dread Dilemma*; *Sex Talk*. Film: *Cherps*.

Dona Croll *Maria Maudlin / Ingrid the Homeless Woman / Citizen*

Theatre credits include: *Elmina's Kitchen* (Bill Kenwright/Royal National Theatre); *Two Step* (Almeida Theatre); *Henry V* (RSC/Tour); *Back Pay* (Royal

Court); *No Boys Cricket Club, Hansel and Gretel* (Theatre Royal, Stratford East); *Victor and the Ladies, Smile Orange* (Tricycle); *Anthony and Cleopatra* (Talawa); *Joe Turner's Come and Gone* (Tricycle); *The City Wives Confederacy, Othello* (Greenwich); *Serious Money* (Wyndhams); *Merchant of Venice* (Royal Exchange); *A Mouthful of Birds* (Joint Stock/Royal Court); *God's Second in Command* (Royal Court Upstairs); *Golden Girls* (West Yorkshire Playhouse); *Back to Methuselah, Polly* (Cambridge Theatre Company); *The Relapse, Jelly Roll Soul* (Lyric, Hammersmith); *It's a Mad House* (Crucible); *The Old Order* (Birmingham Rep); *Jericho, Gin Trap* (Young Vic); *Nine Night* (The Bush). Televison credits include: *Doctors; EastEnders; The Shadow in the North; Time Trumpet; Little Miss Jocelyn;The Last Will and Testament of Billy Two Sheds; Dr Who; Silent Witness; Bremner, Bird and Fortune; William and Mary; Treasure; Family Affairs; The Murder of Stephen Lawrence; Gimme Gimme Gimme; The Bill; Brothers and Sisters; Loving Hazel; Chandler & Co; Birds of a Feather; Casualty; Between the Lines; Us Girls; Desmonds; Surgical Spirit; Rides; Hallelujah Anyhow; Troublemakers; The Paradise Club; The Real Eddie English; Some day Man; Ebony; Black Silk; The 6 O'Clock Show; Come to Mecca; Nations Health; The Boys from the Black Stuff.* Film credits include: *David Cronenberg Project; Kill Kill Faster Faster; I Could Never Be Your Woman; Tube Tales: Rosebud; Manderlay.*

Nadine Marshall *Dona / Citizen / Woman 1 / Passenger / Station Attendant*

Theatre credits include: *Trade* (RSC/Soho Theatre); *Born Bad* (Hampstead Theatre); *Shoot To Win* (Theatre Royal Stratford East); *The Homelife of Polar Bears* (Royal Court Theatre); *The Last Valentine* (Almeida Theatre); *Oroonoko* (RSC); *Timon of Athens* (RSC); *Henry VIII* (RSC); *Spanish Tragedy* (RSC); *Camino Real* (RSC); *The Shining* (Royal Court Theatre). Radio credits include: *The Thebans* (BBC Radio 3); *The #1 Ladies Detective Agency* (BBC Radio); *The Moon Is Mine* (BBC Radio); *Weathering The Storm* (BBC Radio); *Measure For Measure* (BBC Radio); *Solomon Girl* (BBC Radio); *Oroonoko* (BBC Radio). Television credits include: *The Commander; Judge John Deed; Spoil; Trial and Retribution; Jackanory; Little Miss Jocelyn; The Smoking Room; The Bill; Family Affairs.* Film credits include: *These Times; Club Le Monde.*

Mark Monero *Robbie Wedderburn / Drunk / Alastair the Passenger / Citizen 1 / Punter 3 / Citizen*

Theatre credits include: *Sing Yer Heart Out for the Lads* (Pilot Theatre Company); *The Country Wife* (Watford Palace); *Animal* (Red Room/ Soho Theatre); *Adrenalin Heart* (Bush); *Abyssinia* (Southwark Playhouse); *Pepper Soup* (Lyric, Hammersmith); *Talking About Men* (Oval House and Green Room, Manchester); *Local Boy* (Hampstead); *Invisible*

Man (Kings Head); *Warriors in Wasteland* (New End); *A Taste of Honey* (Liverpool Playhouse). Television includes: *Skins*; *Trial and Retribution*; *Doctors*; *Waking the Dead*; *Murphy's Law*; *Judge John Deed*; *Casualty*; *Gimme Gimme Gimme*; *The Bill*; *EastEnders*; *Paradise Club*; *A Wanted Man*; *The Firm*. Film credits include: *Wilt*; *Sid and Nancy*; *Babylon*.

Javone Prince
Kingston the Warden / Greg / Jason / Bohemian / Citizen 2 / Punter 1 / Passenger / Citizen

Theatre credits include: *Out of the Fog* (Almeida Theatre); *Sugar Mummies* (Royal Court); *Burn, Chatroom, Citizenship* (National Theatre); *93.2 FM* (Royal Court); *Raisin in the Sun* (Young Vic and tour); *Car Thieves* (Birmingham Rep); *Titus Andronicus, Richard III, Measure for Measure* (RSC). Television credits include: *Angelo's*; *The Verdict*; *Little Miss Jocelyn*; *What's Going On*; *Murder Prevention*; *My Family*. Film credits include: *The Tiger and the Snow*; *Dommeren*; *Manderlay*. Radio credits include: *Lacy's War*; *Small Island*.

Company

Paulette Randall *Director*

Paulette's career to date has been a mixture of theatre directing and television producing – with some writing thrown in. Most recently she was at Arena Stage in Washington DC directing her second production of August Wilson's *Gem of the Ocean*. Other recent credits include: *Diamond Hard* (Almeida Theatre); *What's in the Cat* (Contact, Manchester /Royal Court); *Gem of the Ocean* (The Tricycle); *The Three Sisters* (Birmingham Rep/ national tour). As Artistic Director of Talawa Theatre, Paulette directed: *Urban Afro Saxons* (Theatre Royal, Stratford East); *Blest be the Tie* (Royal Court); *Abena's Stupidest Mistake* (Drill Hall); *Blues for Mr Charlie* (New Wolsey Ipswich/ Tricycle); *High Heel Parrotfish* (Theatre Royal, Stratford East). Other theatre credits include August Wilson's *The Piano Lesson*; *Two Trains Running*; *King Hedley II;* and the musical *Up Against the Wall* for which she also co-wrote the book. All these were produced at The Tricycle. Television credits include *Desmonds*; *The Real McCoy*; *Porkpie*; *Marvin* (pilot); *Comin' Atcha*; *Blouse and Skirt* (producer/director); *The Crouches*; *Kerching* for the BBC. Paulette is Chairman of the Board for Clean Break Theatre Company.

Libby Watson *Designer*

Libby trained at Bristol Old Vic and Wimbledon School of Art. Design credits include: *Blonde Bombshells of 1943* (Hampstead Theatre/Bolton and UK tour); *French Lieutenant's Woman* (UK tour); *Macbeth* (Bristol Old Vic); *Under their Influence, Blues for Mr Charlie, Gem of the Ocean, The War Next Door* (Tricycle); *Crooked, I like Mine With a Kiss* (Bush); *The Wills's Girls* (Tobacco Factory); *Blest Be the Tie, What's in the Cat* (Royal

Court); *Man of Mode, Hysteria* (Northcott Exeter); *Aladdin* (Bury St Edmunds Theatre Royal); *The Key Game* and *Deranged Marriage* (Riverside Studios); *The Changeling, Beautiful Thing, Arabian Nights, Side By Side by Sondheim, Secret Garden, Tenant of Wildfell Hall* (as resident designer, Salisbury Playhouse); *Ready or Not, Night of the Dons, Cinderella, Jamaica House, Urban Afro Saxons, Sus, High Heeled Parrotfish, Funny Black Women* and *The Oddest Couple* (Stratford East); over ten touring productions for the Watermill Theatre including *I Dreamt I Dwelt in Marble Halls* and *The Comedian*; ten productions for Guildhall including *Merchant of Venice, Twelve Angry Men, Corpus Christi, Three Sisters, Hysteria* (Birmingham Rep). Opera Credits include: *Beatrice and Benedict, Comedy on the Bridge, Mignon* (Guildhall); *National Opera Showcase* (Hackney Empire).

John Bishop
Lighting Designer

John has created original lighting designs for more than a hundred and thirty shows, ballets and operas including: *Milkshake* (Five TV); *Dracula* (Northern Ballet Theatre); *Swan Lake, Cinderella* and *The Nutcracker* (Russian Classical Ballet of the Ukraine); *Sleeping Beauty, Snow White* and *The Nutcracker* (Kiev Classical Ballet); *House of the Gods* (Music Theatre Wales); *Whirlwind* (Streetwise Opera); *Ernani* (English National Opera); *The Most Beautiful Man from* the Sea, La Traviata, Cinderella, West Side Story, A Song of Streets (Welsh National Opera); *Der Ring des Nibelungen, Der Fliegende Holländer* (Den Norske Opera, Oslo); *Peter Grimes, Le Revenant* (Teatro Lirico Nacional, Madrid); *Don Giovanni* (Teatro Alfa & Municipal Theatre, São Paulo); *Cosi Fan Tutte, Falstaff, The Cunning Little Vixen, Don Giovanni, Tosca, Hänsel und Gretel* (Opera Zuid, Maastricht); *Hänsel und Gretel* (Opera Northern Ireland); *Armide, The Fair Maid of Perth, Pimpinone, The Merry Wives of Windsor, Ascanio in Alba, The Barber of Seville, Hercules, Il turco in Italia, Semele, Maria Padilla, Hansel and Gretel, La Périchole, Un giorno di Regno, Fierrabras* (Buxton Festival); *Paul Bunyan, Eugene Onegin, Le Comte Ory, The Rake's Progress, La Bohème, The Knot Garden, Suor Angelica, L'Heure Espagnol, Albert Herring* (Royal College of Music); *The Marriage of Figaro* (The Guildhall and Lyric Theatre, Hammersmith); *The Marriage of Figaro, Jekyll & Hyde, The Fairy Queen, Dr.Dee, Merrily We Roll Along, The Cunning Little Vixen, Fiddler on the Roof, La Calisto, Pygmallion, Dido & Aeneas* (Birmingham Conservatoire); *The Boy who Kicked Pigs, Frankenstein, Psycho, The Queen Who Didn't Come to Tea, When the Earth Sings* (Scottish Chamber Orchestra); *Brand* (The Aldwych Theatre); the rock opera *Demones* in Athens; *The Woman in Black* in Dubai. Future plans include lighting designs for *Bluebeard, Roberto Devereaux* and *Romeo and Juliet* for Buxton Festival and *Romeo and Juliet* and *The Nutcracker* for the Ukraine National Ballet.

Dan Steele *Sound Designer*

Sound design work for theatre includes: *Clockwork* (Breaking Cycles/The Royal National Theatre); *Mother Courage and Her Children*, *Hamlet* (with West End transfer), *The Old Country* (with West End transfer), *Rosencrantz and Guildenstern are Dead* (English Touring Theatre); *What's in the Cat*, (Contact/The Royal Court); *Smilin' Through* (Birmingham Rep/Contact); *Bro:9* (Manchester Evening News Award for Best Design 2003), *Perfect* (Manchester Evening News Award for Best Design 2004), *You Hang Up First*, *Under My Skin* (Contact); *13 Mics*, *B Like Water* (Benji Reid Company). Sound design/ composition for film and Television includes: *Bro:9* (B3 media and British Film Council); *Fred and Rose West* (MMA productions).

Susannah Henry
Costume Designer

Susannah Henry trained in theatre design at Wimbledon School of Art and Central Saint Martins College of Art and Design. Recent design work includes: *C-90* (Riverside Studios, Traverse Theatre and currently on tour); *Inherit the Wind* (Guildhall); *Mary Kelly's Bed*, *The Crowning of the Year*, *You Make Me Happy When Skies Are Grey* (Watermill Theatre); *Shiver* (Pleasance and UK Tour); *Sweet Yam Kisses* (Lyric Hammersmith). Susannah

lectures in Stage Design on the MA Scenography for Dance programme at Laban and is Associate Design tutor at Mountview Academy of Theatre Arts.

Antoinette Lester
Assistant Director

Antoinette graduated from the University of Wolverhampton having studied a BA in Theatre and English Literature. Theatre credits include: *My Mother Said I Never Should*, *Shakespeare's Women* and *Shakespeare's Little Black Book*, *Lysistrata* (Assistant Director), *Miss Julie* (Arena Theatre Woverhampton) In 2005, Antoinette graduated from Rose Bruford College having completed a masters degree, specialising in directing. During her year of study she co-directed *Jack* (Rose Theatre), devised and directed *Autumn Of His Years* (Kinematic works company/Rose Bruford studios), *When The Lights Go Out* (Rose Bruford Studios) and directed a new adaptation of *Medea* (Barn Theatre) for Black History Month.

● soho theatre

- Produces new work
- Discovers and nurtures new writers
- Targets and develops new audiences

Soho Theatre creates and enables daring and original new work that challenges the status quo by igniting the imaginations of writers, artists and audiences. We initiate new conversations with London and the wider world through projects that celebrate creative participation, internationalism and freedom of expression. We nurture socially and culturally broad audiences for theatre and create a buzz around theatre as a living and relevant art form.

'a foundry for new talent... one of the country's leading producers of new writing' Evening Standard

Soho Theatre has a unique Writers' Centre which offers an invaluable resource to emerging theatre writers. The nation's only unsolicited script-reading service, we report for free on over 2,000 plays per year. Through the Verity Bargate Award, the Writers' Attachment Programme, and a host of development programmes and workshops we aim to develop groundbreaking writers and artists to broaden the definition of new theatre writing. Our learning and participation programme Soho Connect includes the innovative Under 11's scheme, the Young Writers' Group (18-25s), Script Slam and an annual site-specific theatre piece with the local community.

Alongside our theatre productions, Soho Theatre presents a high profile late night programme with a mixture of groundbreaking comedy and performance from leading and emergent artists. We also curate talks and other events, encouraging the conversation to spill over into our new and reasonably priced Soho Theatre Bar.

Contemporary, comfortable, air-conditioned and accessible, Soho Theatre is busy from early morning to late at night.

'London's coolest theatre by a mile' Midweek

● soho theatre

Soho Theatre, 21 Dean St, London W1D 3NE
Admin: 020 7287 5060 Box Office: 0870 429 6883
www.sohotheatre.com

Soho Theatre Bar

The new Soho Theatre Bar is a comfortable and affordable place to meet in central London.

The Terrace Bar

The Terrace Bar on the second floor serves a range of soft and alcoholic drinks.

Email information list

For regular programme updates and offers visit www.sohotheatre.com

Hiring the theatre

Soho Theatre has a range of rooms and spaces for hire. Please contact the theatre managers on 020 7287 5060 or go to www.sohotheatre.com for further details.

● soho theatre

THE SOHO THEATRE DEVELOPMENT CAMPAIGN

Soho Theatre receives core funding from Arts Council England, London. In order to provide as diverse a programme as possible and expand our audience development and outreach work, we rely upon additional support from trusts, foundations, individuals and businesses.

All of our major sponsors share a common commitment to developing new areas of activity and encouraging creative partnerships between business and the arts.

We are immensely grateful for the invaluable support from our sponsors and donors and wish to thank them for their continued commitment.

Soho Theatre has a Friends Scheme in support of its education programme and work developing new writers and reaching new audiences. To find out how to become a Friend of Soho Theatre, contact the development department on 020 7478 0109, email development@sohotheatre.com or visit www.sohotheatre.com.

Sponsors: Angels The Costumiers, Arts & Business, Bloomberg, International Asset Management, Rathbones, TEQUILA\ London

Major Supporters and Education Patrons: Tony and Rita Gallagher • Nigel Gee • Paul Hamlyn Foundation • Roger Jospé • Jack and Linda Keenan • John Lyon's Charity • The Pemberton Foundation • The Foundation for Sport and the Arts • Carolyn Ward • The Harold Hyam Wingate Foundation • The City Bridge Trust

Soho Business Members: Goodman Derrick • ilovesoho.com

Trusts and Foundations: Anonymous • The Andor Charitable Trust • The Sydney & Elizabeth Corob Charity • The Earmark Trust • Hyde Park Place Estate Charity • The Mackintosh Foundation • The Rose Foundation • Leopold de Rothschild Charitable Trust • The Royal Victoria Hall Foundation • Saddlers' Company • Teale Charitable Trust • Bruce Wake Charitable Trust • The Kobler Trust • The Carr-Gregory Trust

Dear Friends: Anonymous • Jill and Michael Barrington • David Day • John Drummond • Daniel Friel • Madeleine Hamel • Steve Hill • Michael and Mimi Naughton • Hannah Pierce • Nicola Stanhope • Diana Toeman

Good Friends and Friends: Thank you also to the many Soho Friends we are unable to list here. For a full list of our patrons, please visit www.sohotheatre.com

Registered Charity: 267234

THE CHRIST OF COLDHARBOUR LANE

First published in 2007 by Oberon Books Ltd
521 Caledonian Road, London N7 9RH
Tel: 020 7607 3637 / Fax: 020 7607 3629
e-mail: info@oberonbooks.com
www.oberonbooks.com

A catalogue record for this book is available from the British
Library.

Cover illustration by Bryon Fear

ISBN: 1 84002 785 1 / 978 1 84002 785 3

Characters

OMOTUNDE (OMO): British-Nigerian, late twenties

SARAH: Black-British, late twenties

GREG: Black-British, mid-thirties

MARIA MAUDLIN: Black-British, early forties

KINGSTON: Jamaican, early sixties

DONA: Black-British, late twenties

JASON: Black-British, mid-thirties

ROBBIE WEDDERBURN: Black-British, late twenties

CITIZENS OF BRIXTON: BOHEMIAN, DRUNK, WOMAN, PUNTERS, ETC

UNDERGROUND PASSENGERS

The Christ of Coldharbour Lane

Autumn, bordering on winter.

Soundscape: Street noises, loud music from passing vehicles, police sirens.

Outside Brixton Prison, which is represented by a pole with a roll of barbed wire around it and a CCTV camera on top of it. The sets are placed on stage by passers-by from whom emerge OMO, DONA and KINGSTON. OMO is dressed casually in jeans, shirt and a jacket. At his feet lies a box containing his possessions. DONA wears a sweater with the words 'Prisoners for Christ' on it. She holds a bag containing DVDs, tracts, books. OMO surveys his surroundings as if he is experiencing the world for the first time. KINGSTON, the prison warden, drinks from a bottle of water. He glares at OMO. His glare dissolves into a smile whenever he faces DONA. He wipes his eyes intermittently. DONA looks at OMO as if he is her pet dog and has won first prize at Crufts.

DONA: (*To OMO.*) Lovely bed-sit we've got for you, Brother Omo. Guess where?

OMO: On Coldharbour Lane?

DONA nods triumphantly.

Thank you Sister Dona.

DONA: Brixton's gone all toney since you've been away. It's all the new money moving in. (*Rummages through her bag.*) You can't tell the difference between the high street and any other high street. Except for that buzz. That's one thing you'll never bleach out of Brixton.

OMO: That is good to know.

DONA: Doesn't matter how many trendy bars and chain stores they put up: you know you're in Brixton. I didn't give you my folder, did I?

OMO shakes his head.

I must have left it at the front desk. One minute. (*Exits.*)

OMO bends down and wipes his hands on the ground. He looks at his palms with wondrous appreciation.

KINGSTON: That girl's flightiness make her deaf. I warn her about you and still she is helping you.

OMO: (*Still looking at his palms.*) Sorry?

KINGSTON: Your smile of deceit cannot hide your madness. In her presence you is pretending that she have convert you. Behind her back you preach heresy.

OMO: You call it heresy to justify locking me up. For three years your walls have held a political prisoner.

KINGSTON: You were locked up for impersonating the Prime Minister. You is Rory Bremner? You so stupid you didn't even chalk up your face. Is no wonder Dr Gupta say you is mad.

OMO: How do you know what he said? That's confidential information.

KINGSTON: I have ears that overhear. I've seen you impersonate me. Even a mimic has his own personality. But you! You swallow a person body and soul.

OMO: I was in the spirit.

KINGSTON: Oh, is dat why you refused to leave your cell claiming dat you is hearing voices?

OMO: Rapture is mistaken for madness. Dr Gupta works for the establishment. Naturally he would hide the truth from the world.

KINGSTON: Ah so? I never see dem pump so much Largactil into a man. If not for Dona you would still be in the psychiatric ward. She don't know she is helping the devil to do his work.

OMO: I work for the Father. I came first on the 'Born Anew' programme.

KINGSTON: Exam standards aren't what dey used to be. Your wotless certificate doesn't give you the licence to call yourself even a false prophet.

OMO: I have honour in my home town. I will return to my people. They will acknowledge me.

KINGSTON: Is obeah you use on Dona or juju is why she believe you is from Brixton? Your home is a mud hut Bob Geldof can't find time feh visit. Is just dat I'm feeling lucky; I woulda bet my pools coupon dat you is an illegal immigrant. Dey should have ship you straight to Heat'row.

OMO: The world is my Father's temple. Coldharbour Lane is my home.

KINGSTON: Me can't believe. From Prime Minister you graduate to Christ! Chris Rock say dere is black man and dere is nigger. I never agree with him before. Nigger is the filthiest word to come from a black man mouth. Is you he was talking about. Lock up is too good for you. I don't know why the police didn't kill you in custody.

OMO: Your eyes are blinded and your heart hardened. I am your redeemer. Believe in me, for my Father has committed everything into my hands.

KINGSTON: I is a God-fearing Christian! Don't quote the Bible to me you son of a perverse rebellious woman.

OMO: Are you the one crying in the wilderness?

KINGSTON: You is an offence to humanity to ask me that question. Move from here! (*Shoves OMO.*)

OMO: (*Catches KINGSTON's hands.*) The thought that a black man could be your saviour repulses you. Deny your self-hatred. (*Tries to lay a hand on KINGSTON's head.*)

KINGSTON: Lay that hand on me and you will see black on black violence! (*Breaks free of OMO's grasp. Whacks OMO's other hand away from his head.*) Go preach your lunacy to your African brethren. I seen deir video flim. Is dem believe in all kinda voodoo. Why you don't say you is a reincarnation of Shango? Why is the white man's ting you always have feh mash up?

OMO: Your eyes are blinded and your heart is hardened by the establishment.

KINGSTON: Who is your father? Who gave birth to you, you foundling?

OMO: I am the son of my Father!

A bell rings.

Alfred! His is the voice crying in the wilderness.

KINGSTON: Town crier Alfie Howard? Alfie dead. Is the town hall clock ringing. Your ears are deaf to reality, and you expect people to believe your falsehood.

OMO: What can I do to make you believe?

KINGSTON: Me is a New Labour focus group? All right, if you're who you say you are walk on water. Go on, walk across the Thames let me see you.

OMO: You seek a sign to take for a wonder?

KINGSTON: (*Brings out a bottle of water.*) I'll make it easier for you. Turn this water into rum. Appleton, not Malibu. Come on, what you waiting for?

OMO: Man of little faith.

KINGSTON: (*Tastes the water.*) Me thought as much.

OMO: My people will acknowledge me, those who have been left behind. They have no need for a sign. For too long they have been waiting for the truth. Be assured: I will fulfil my destiny.

KINGSTON: Your destiny is to roast in hell. Me willing to send you dere! (*Approaches OMO to assault him.*)

DONA enters. KINGSTON retreats and smiles at her like nothing's going on.

18

DONA: (*Waves the file.*) OK. Are we ready?

OMO: I'm ready.

DONA: Later Kingston. God bless. (*Exits.*)

KINGSTON: God bless, Dona. See you tomorrow.

OMO and DONA exit.

Walter Mitty fantasist. (*Looks after him.*)

Can you believe that fool? Is mad him mad you know.
Nobody will believe his stupidness... But I bet on England
winning the World Cup. Ah, is not the same thing.

Roadside PREACHERS, spreading their messages, appear.

But dere's something in his eyes. If you stare at him too
long he can make you believe anything. He don't affect
me because me have glaucoma. Don't tell me employers.
Pensions don't go far these days. All dem hardened
criminals he got to join The Mission before him start him
madness. And then a smart girl like Dona believe him
when him say him cured. Dr Gupta believe him too. Prince
Philip talk the truth. Indians, dem useless as engineers and
dem wotless as psychiatrists too... And him preaching
all kindsa nonsense behind Dona back, sounding like a
bloody communist. I'm not surprised...

Changes his clothes to GREG's.

... If there's one thing Moslems and Christians agree on
is that communists are heretics. Is what trouble-makers
become when dem don't know deir place. Dey think dey
can turn the world upside down so that dey can become
boss. Is my duty as a Christian and a patriot ah dis country
to report him to the authorities. I better call Greg. He
knows people in high places and he wants to join dem up
dere. Ever since him graduate from Oxford him have dis
overbearing sense of entitlement. Young people nowadays,
you too impatient. Learn from the Prince of Wales. If he
was like Greg he woulda poison his mother by now. Me

nephew turn down an assignment just because dey want him to do a feature on Brixton.

KINGSTON turns into GREG.

GREG: That's because it's typical that they'd give their only black reporter the job. How should I know what it's like living in an inner city? I live in Muswell Hill for God's sake. The South Bank's as far as I go south of the river. I went to school with guys who're moving up in high places. I can get access to the stories that matter if you put me on the right assignment. (*Sighs with resignation.*) I might as well take Uncle Kingston's advice. Start from the bottom and work my way up. I bet the Duke of Westminster never had that problem. Luck of the draw.

The scene morphs into Brixton High Street.

Roadside PREACHERS spreading their messages. GREG takes in the scene.

God, like moths to light. There must be something in the water. I'm wasting my time chasing up on Uncle Kingston's self-proclaimed messiah. I mean, take your pick. I need another angle and fast so I can get the hell out of here... Wow, Brixton's got a metro. (*Heads off in the direction of the metro.*)

Soundscape: Noises of the street.

Coldharbour Lane, Brixton. OMO and DONA are engulfed by the CITIZENS OF BRIXTON (the roadside preachers of the previous scene) who set up OMO's bed-sit as they act as passers-by on the street: a chair, a single bed, a table, a small cupboard on the table, a TV and a DVD player. SARAH, in a wheelchair, wheels by. GREG, with a camcorder, wanders around looking for something interesting to shoot. SARAH and GREG do not notice each other.

DONA: Not too far, we're almost there. (*To a CITIZEN OF BRIXTON.*) Excuse me.

CITIZEN moves out of DONA's way. As DONA and OMO enter the bed-sit, CITIZENS exit as if they are passers-by on the street. Inside the bed-sit. Street noises subside.

DONA: Here we are. What do you think?

OMO: It is very nice.

DONA: (*Unpacks her bag.*) Ready meals in the fridge. And I got you some more copies of *Prayer Request Live.* (*Hands him the DVDs.*) Thank God for Bit Torrent, eh!

OMO: Thanks.

OMO opens the window. The sounds of the street.

DONA: (*Puts away the provisions.*) Hope you're not an afternoon sleeper. You'll have to swallow a bottle of valium to even close your eyelids in this racket... I'm sorry. I didn't mean to say that.

OMO: (*Closes the window.*) I didn't think you were referring to Largactil, Sister Dona. Don't look like that.

DONA: I of all people should be sensitive to your past.

OMO: It's OK.

DONA: Dad says I run at the mouth.

OMO: An essential quality in an evangelist. You are to the collar born.

DONA: Ha! Imagine me, a Catholic priest. Confessions would be public knowledge with my big mouth. With The Mission gender's no barrier to becoming a minister. Did I tell you? I just heard this morning: I've made the shortlist again for the next promotions. I've impressed the church elders with my Prisoners Reform Programme. With you being released today is a good day all round.

OMO: There is a lot to be cheerful for.

DONA: Imagine you, my protégé rising through the ranks too. You'll be my right hand man. That's got to be worth a few more brownie points for me.

OMO: It would be worth something.

DONA: I have to comport myself in a right manner from now on. I'm not getting turned down this time just because I can't keep my mouth shut. You'll be my full stop whenever I rattle on. We'll make a great team. South London won't know what's hit it.

OMO: I can't wait for tomorrow. We shall turn Brixton into our Father's citadel.

DONA: (*Unpacks OMO's box. Hands OMO his certificate.*) I'm glad The Elders finally agreed for you to partner me. They wanted me to go with a more experienced missionary. I don't blame them. Our recruitment drive hasn't taken off in Brixton. You saw the high street. It isn't short of competition.

OMO: I did not win this (*Shows her the certificate.*) for nothing. If I can convert people inside prison, I can convert people anywhere.

DONA: Exactly what I told the elders. Your talent for reaching people's souls makes up for your inexperience. It's those eyes of yours. No one can resist them.

OMO: The eyes are the window to the soul. Once I open the eyes of the people the choice is already made. They will hear the word.

DONA: Wonderful. Preach like you did back in prison, we'll be on the way up.

OMO: Thank you for having faith in me. I shall not disappoint you. The people of Brixton shall accept the Second Coming.

DONA: Good, because you'll need to move the earth just to get their attention, never mind convert them. Our survey shows that Brixtonians are preached to on average twelve times a day. They learn of a new religion twice a month. And they hear preaching from six denominations every

day. And that's just between Coldharbour Lane and
Electric Avenue.

OMO: Why all the statistics?

DONA: It's good to know who you're competing with. Not
for any other reason than to help us get the true message
across. You've seen the high street. It's like a stock market
pit.

OMO: But the word spreads. I was pleasantly stunned to see
those Chinese evangelicals by the junction. The Lord is
reaching the places where communism cannot reach.

DONA: (*Disdainful.*) Korean.

OMO: Eh?

DONA: They're Korean.

OMO: Oh, North Korean.

DONA: I don't know. Everyone's getting in on the act. Forget
Jerusalem and Mecca. Brixton is the most religious place
on earth. Not a bad thing in itself only the people are
getting jaded. If Christ landed in Tate Gardens for his
Second Coming, Brixtonians would be like, 'Join the
queue'.

OMO: I can convince them. They will recognise the Lord in
their midst.

DONA: That's what I want to hear. I don't deal in failure
where the Lord is concerned and He is concerned with
everything. People must remember that this is a Christian
country.

OMO: Surely everyone knows that.

DONA: You'd have thought. Christianity is the whipping boy of
the chattering classes. You'd be amazed at how many times
we're slated by the liberal press. I'd like to see them attack
Islam the same way. Dad says that's the reason why this
country's gone to the dogs. The foundation's broken.

OMO: Your father is a big influence on you.

DONA: Yes, I… There I go again! What is wrong with me today? I'm pressing all the wrong buttons.

OMO: It's all right, I'm not offended. You're quite comfortable inside your skin. That's a good thing. Not everyone is so secure about themselves.

DONA: Yes but I can be so inconsiderate.

OMO: I said don't worry about it. You seem close to your father.

DONA: Yeah, the old stuck up. I love him anyway. I'm Daddy's little girl and the lastborn in my family so I had it easy with the old dragon.

OMO: He's your link to the past.

DONA: Mm, my Mum says I'm just like him. I hope not. I mean, he's solid C of E. He doesn't think much of The Mission. 'Your preaching is junk food for the soul.' He believes what he's read in the papers that we're a cult. Something profound happens to you, it should transform you, right? You accepted the Lord and hasn't it changed you for the better? Don't you feel like a new person?

OMO: Completely.

DONA: And what about worshipping the Lord with all your heart and mind and soul? Who wants to sit in some cold church listening to a man in robes droning on? Reverend Williams has done great work in bringing the Lord's riches to us. Hello! We're in the twenty-first century. No one wants to live in penury. If any one is going to turn this country around it's going to be people like you and me.

OMO: I know.

DONA: Dad doesn't get it. He's still living in the seventies. Um, sorry I keep mentioning him every minute.

OMO: Don't be. So long as the Father loves me I am not an orphan.

DONA: That's what The Mission is all about: all of us coming together in God's family. I'll leave you to settle in. Oh, did I get you the *Good News* handbook?

OMO holds up the handbook.

Great, you can brush up on your skills. Get ready to convert Brixton and then the world.

OMO: I am ready for the world. Is the world ready for me?

DONA: Sorry?

OMO: A joke, Sister Dona.

DONA: Oh. It's just that Kingston said…oh never mind. He never really liked you, did he?

OMO: Kingston is a bitter man. He knew I was abandoned at birth. You didn't by accident let slip…

DONA: I'd never tell him anything like that about you.

OMO: Christ was born in a manger.

DONA: Forget Kingston. You cannot be anything other than God's child. The Mission is your family. Who knows, your impersonations may come in handy. We do all kinds of entertainment at our fundraisers… Oh come here. (*Hugs him. She pulls away and brings out the chain around OMO's neck. The pendant is a piece of rock.*) I thought you'd done away with all this.

OMO: I have. I kept it to remind me of my past.

DONA: Where's the rest?

OMO reluctantly goes to his box and brings out an ankle bracelet, a white handkerchief and a white caftan.

DONA: (*Reaches for them.*) I'd better take these.

OMO: No! I'll throw them away myself. It is only right that I should. I am a new person. *I am.*

DONA: This is one impersonation you carried too far, Brother Omo. You are not a spirit child.

OMO: I know.

DONA: There is no celestial church that can save you from a silly life and death cycle.

OMO: I know, I know.

DONA: What about your crucifix?

OMO brings out a crucifix from his pocket.

DONA: Brother Omo!

OMO: (*Puts it around his neck.*) The rock is around my neck but the Lord is always on my mind.

DONA: Uh-huh. I'm not sure I buy that.

OMO: Revelations 21:19 to 20. The stones that are the bedrock of Jerusalem. We are the foundation of the New Jerusalem here in Brixton. First Brixton, then the world.

DONA: Trust you to find an answer for everything. OK, see you tomorrow.

OMO: Tomorrow, Sister Dona.

DONA: (*Points to the handkerchief, caftan and bracelet.*) And you will...?

OMO: (*Removes his rock pendant, puts it with the handkerchief, caftan and bracelet and gathers them up.*) Certainly.

DONA hesitates by the door. She exits. OMO leaves the handkerchief, caftan and bracelet. He takes off the crucifix and puts it back in his pocket and puts the rock pendant back around his neck. OMO flicks through the handbook unenthusiastically. He puts it on the table. He puts the Prayer Request Live *DVD on. As the DVD plays, OMO changes his top. On his chest is a marking, resembling the cross.*

26

DVD: (*In a Southern American drawl.*) Ask the Lord, He will answer your prayers. He will transform your lives. Touch the screen. Touch the screen. Bob in Utah needs a new car. God is answering your prayer right now. Mrs Baker in Houston, God is curing your son of his homosexuality as we speak.

OMO goes down on his knees. He mimics Reverend Williams:

Touch the screen. Touch the screen. Jose in New York is asking for the return of prayers in school. Eugene in Ohio, a million dollars is coming your way today in Jesus' name. Amen and amen.

That's all on *Prayer Request Live*, folks. Remember: we are all God's children. Ask our Father whatever you want. Belief is the key that unlocks the door to heavenly and earthly riches. We will create a new world in the image God wants us to, a new world of prosperity for all his children. Until next time, this is Reverend Williams saying, stay blessed and stay with The Mission. (*Music.*)

OMO recovers. Then, he sways as he feels himself being pulled one way and then another. He reaches for the bracelet of cowries and puts it around his ankle. The sound of a baby crying is punctuated by singing in Yoruba of the Celestial Church, followed by frantic praying. OMO calms down. His demeanour changes to sober realisation. He takes the handbook and throws it in the bin. The praying fades out.

The music of the DVD continues as the citizens of Brixton change the set. The music fades into the noises of Brixton High Street.

The following day, outside Brixton Station. People going to work. DONA and OMO preaching. DONA hands out tracts. CITIZENS pass by, ignoring them.

DONA: (*Preaching.*) God loves you so much he gave his only son! (*To a CITIZEN.*) Brother, do you want everlasting happiness? All you have to do is accept Christ as your Lord and saviour...

OMO: You must wipe your soul of sin before you can enter the kingdom. Shed your skin of your sins.

DONA: (*Unsurely looking at OMO.*) All else shall be added on to you. He has forgiven you even before you've sinned. Accept Christ and the riches of the earth shall follow.

OMO: Nothing comes except through the son. Transform yourselves, cast off your earthly possessions.

DONA: (*To a CITIZEN.*) Brother. Brother! One second. Don't be shy. (*CITIZEN approaches cautiously. DONA presses a leaflet into his hand.*) I'm with The Mission, the true gateway to Heaven. We've over seven thousand members in London alone, saved for Heaven and prospering on earth.

OMO: Prepare to enter the New Jerusalem. Leave your earthly desires at the gates.

CITIZEN leaves, dropping the leaflet.

DONA: Brother, wait! Brother Omo, let's catch a break.

OMO: It is easier for a camel to pass through...

DONA: Brother Omo.

OMO: ...the eye of a needle than for a rich man to enter the kingdom!

DONA: Brother Omo! Break. Now.

OMO: (*Looks at his watch.*) Um, OK, if that is what you want.

DONA: Did you catch up on the handbook?

OMO: I watched the DVD.

DONA: I asked you whether you revised with the handbook. That was my question /

OMO: I picked it up but I felt like I was back in prison.

DONA: Why on earth should it make you feel that way? Have you been reading the material of another church?

OMO: No.

DONA: So what's with the 'eye of the needle'? What happened to our Good News Approach?

OMO: I'm not sure we are preparing the people properly.

DONA: We haven't exactly signed up any one to prepare.

OMO: I think we're giving the wrong impression. We should be letting people know that the road ahead is hard. They will have to shake off their old lives entirely.

DONA: You're starting to sound like my Dad. That is so old school. God's love is unconditional otherwise we'd all be on a budget flight to hell because we've all fallen short. God knows I have. Christ died for us because he knew we cannot help but sin. You can try to be like Christ but you can never be Christ.

OMO: Then we must try.

DONA: You can't turn yourself inside out. You still have to live in the world and give unto the Chancellor what is the Chancellor's. Remember, we're lambs in the midst of wolves.

OMO: Reforming ourselves completely, that is our only way to break the cycle, to change the world. All these wandering souls, looking for a way out of the wilderness of their humdrum lives; they will follow the true leader if only they hear his voice.

DONA: And they won't hear his voice if we can't get them into our service.

OMO: But when they hear me tell them the truth /

DONA: (*Jokingly.*) You're not going to impersonate Reverend Williams, are you?

OMO is not amused by her comment.

Sorry! Not funny. I must admit though: on my own I'd have signed up a fair few new converts by now.

OMO: With your Good News gospel of prosperity for nothing.

DONA: Not for nothing. They have to become active members of The Mission before the good things come to them.

OMO: I feel we are tending more to material needs.

DONA: Ye-ah. The body and soul are one. Connect with the body the soul is yours for the taking. You've never sat through a sermon on an empty stomach.

OMO: This is not Darfur. I doubt that many people go hungry.

DONA: Our God is not a poor God. Everything on this earth belongs to Him. God's children, me, you and all who believe, are the rightful owners of the world down to the bricks and mortar. Those left out are those who by omission or by commission have put their faith either in themselves or in false gods. You've done it before, you know the difference. We're doing a good thing bringing these other prodigals back into the family. We're helping them to claim their share.

OMO: But the spirit of our Father moves me to do more.

DONA: I was just like you when I found Christ. I wanted to convert the whole world. But I had to learn to channel my urge in the right direction. You'll find out how it all works when you train to become a minister. There's a process to acquiring souls.

OMO: This process feels too corporate.

DONA: It isn't corporate. The Good News Approach is psychology-based. People respond to material needs. You responded to it.

A homeless WOMAN sits on the ground, puts her hat down and starts begging.

OMO: Not for material gain. My Father called me and I heeded his voice.

DONA: You're saying that now.

OMO: I have always said it. God considered me according to my need. The call was for me, no one else.

DONA: When I was young my family lived in this small town outside London. Dad dragged me to church every Sunday. The old parish priest was retiring and so they brought in this new priest. Was I happy? For the first time I met a black man in a position of authority. But the parishioners wrote to the Archbishop. They weren't comfortable with him leading the service.

A smartly dressed man passes by. DONA waves to catch his attention. He ignores her and exits.

The next week he was gone. I get your argument. And it's true. We're all special in God's eyes. What you like those parishioners forget is that He also made us the human race – one family. Extend your 'we're all unique' ideology, all you're doing is opening up the world to divisions. In the spirit we are one. If anything you should be happy that we believe in one family.

SARAH passes by.

Sister Sarah! Hold up.

SARAH: Hi Dona.

DONA: Minister Andrews has been trying to contact you. We've not been seeing you in church. What happened?

SARAH: Nothing. That's why I stopped going to service.

DONA: You must keep believing, Sister Sarah. If the Lord wants you to walk again you will walk. But it can't be to your schedule.

SARAH: (*Shrugs.*) Well then.

DONA: Don't be like that. When the time comes, you will be lifted even higher than before.

SARAH: Time is essential in my line of work. And I hear its ticking louder each day.

DONA: Which is why you must never give up hope. Or maybe God has another plan in store for you. You don't want all our prayers to go to waste. Come back to service and we shall work out another prayer plan for your miracle healing.

SARAH: Been there, done that.

DONA: What can I say to make you come back?

SARAH: You've already done all the talking.

DONA: Give yourself another chance with God.

SARAH: You mean give God another chance?

DONA: Sister Sarah! God loves you anyway. The door is always open.

SARAH: I think I'll pass on that.

OMO: Believe.

SARAH: And you are?

DONA: This is Omo. He's my colleague.

SARAH: That's an African name, isn't it?

OMO: Yoruba, from Nigeria. It's short for Omotunde. It means the son returns.

SARAH: Ah. Welcome back.

OMO: Sarah, ask and you shall receive. But first you must believe.

SARAH: (*To DONA.*) You might want to tell your ministers to sort out disabled access.

DONA: Will you come back to us then?

SARAH: Nope.

OMO: First believe, Sarah. First believe.

SARAH looks curiously at OMO. She shakes her head as she exits.

DONA: Well said, Brother Omo. 'Give God a chance.' You get what I'm saying about your 'I'm unique' view? You end up like her, rejecting the Lord, bitter and lonely. I bet when she won her gold medal she thought she was invincible. She's a lesson to be learned from. (*Spots the homeless* WOMAN. *Approaches her.*) Sister! For how long will you stay in the cold when the Lord offers you shelter?

WOMAN: I haven't eaten for a week.

DONA: The Lord will not let his chosen go hungry. (*Opens her purse. Brings out some money.*) How does a nice beef pattie sound?

WOMAN: It don't sound like KFC to me.

DONA: (*Reluctantly digs into her purse for more money.*) The Lord answers your prayer even before you ask.

WOMAN: The Jews, they have English blood you know. Is why Jesus feed the five thousand fish an' chips. But Jesus know if he land in Brixton, is a Family Bucket he hav' feh conjure.

DONA: Have you heard about The Mission?

WOMAN: No but say the word. Who you wan' me feh kill? The mayor? When me nose block me kian buy Vicks because me kian afford di congestion charge.

DONA: No! No. The *Mission*. The Lord's one true church.

WOMAN: Ah, is like Tom Cruise, innit? He hav' feh join Scientology before him get him licence to kill in *Mission Impossible…*

DONA and WOMAN exit.

OMO remains where he is.

The following day.

Rush hour. People going to work, rushing past OMO, leaving him disorientated. Left with OMO are the CITIZENS of Brixton, those left behind: the homeless, the unemployed, the drug dealers, the single mothers pushing their prams. MARIA MAUDLIN, on her way to work. SARAH wheels after MARIA. They freeze. OMO bends down and wipes his hands on the ground.

OMO: The touch of home, my home, Brixistane, where streetlights first lit up the London night, the rock upon which New Jerusalem will be built. Brixton, a great spillover of excessive dreams. Anonymous masses. All of you are dancers of the dying beat. I come with the strong arm to ignite the rhythm, to drive again your passion for life. (*The passers-by and loiterers do not respond. He sighs.*) If only the people will acknowledge me. If only they will claim their birthright as I have done then they will wait in vain no more. I see it in their eyes. They see no reason for reform. Life must go on, but like this? I will fulfil the task the Father has sent me to do and he will be pleased with me. (*Looks around at those left behind.*) I will find my twelve and they will follow me. And then I will take my message to Brixton and to the world.

The town hall bell rings. The CITIZENS unfreeze. As one they look to the town hall clock and then go about their business.

The voice of the one crying in the wilderness! Alfie!

CITIZEN: Where you been, man? Alfie's dead. (*Exits.*)

OMO: (*Breaks out of his reverie.*) Ah, Tate Gardens. Here's where I should be, with my people who need me.

MARIA exits. SARAH tries unsuccessfully to catch her attention. She exits angrily in the opposite direction.

CITIZENS set up Tate Gardens with a bench as OMO walks into the scene. OMO turns round to look at the CITIZENS chilling, drinking, doing drugs. He spots BOHEMIAN, dressed in scruff-bag chic, sitting on a bench. OMO nods at him. BOHEMIAN smiles, beckoning OMO to join him. OMO sits beside him.

BOHEMIAN: Welcome to the One Seat Theatre. Admission is free. To justify my non-funding I need your participation.

OMO: I am not an actor.

BOHEMIAN: Friend, everyone is an actor. I'm Paul.

OMO: Hello Paul. I'm Omo.

BOHEMIAN: For this performance you'll be Peter. Search inside my coat pocket and bring out whatever you find. Go on.

OMO brings out a five pound note.

Now say the line.

OMO: What?

BOHEMIAN: 'I've robbed you, Paul, to pay me, Peter!'

OMO looks in askance.

(*Sighs. Takes back the note.*) An artist is not recognised on his own street. Fame will come. One day.

OMO: You seek fame?

BOHEMIAN: Money, really. I tell you, this starving artist lark is so *fin de siècle*. God knows why I feel guilty about wanting a life. I mean, Brixton itself has had such a facelift my mates aren't terrified of hanging out here any more. I've been holding out against the tide but now I'm holding up my hands. Fame's the easiest way out of poverty. Slap your face on TV for the viewing pleasure of folks and you're on the way to a decent pension plan.

OMO: And if you run out of money?

BOHEMIAN: Turn the other cheek.

OMO: Why?

BOHEMIAN: Don't know about you but I find it galling when I see chancers race up the celebrity ladder to fortune. I've tried to stay true to the profession. It's just not worth it any more. The philistines have scaled the wall. I have no choice but to surrender to the great pay day.

OMO: You would be a slave to mammon? You would dehumanise yourself to line your pocket?

BOHEMIAN: I'm human: anything I do can't be dehumanising. I'll play the game like everyone else.

OMO: But what if you could have a hand in making your own game, play by your own rules?

BOHEMIAN: You pan through the same dirt to get to the gold.

OMO: It's not worth losing your dignity over.

BOHEMIAN: Dignity went out with the socialists. Who were never in, by the way.

OMO: Think about securing a foothold in our new world.

BOHEMIAN: I'm still trying to sort out my life in this world, my dear idealist. Anyway I dirty my body but I keep my soul clean.

OMO: But if I told you that body and soul are inseparable, that one is the other?

BOHEMIAN: I'd say there is one and there's the other. I'd say one thing at a time. I'm not only an actor. I write as well. I don't want to jinx it: I'm waiting to hear from The Royal Court. I sent them my play.

OMO: What is your play called?

BOHEMIAN: *Everything but the Kitchen Sink.* Fingers crossed, it'll be up their street.

OMO: You place faith in uncertainties when I offer you a new life set upon the bedrock. Follow me and as I change the world so shall your desires change. You will become a new person. (*Holds BOHEMIAN.*) I am the rock on which the New Jerusalem will be built.

*ROBBIE WEDDERBURN enters with briefcase and mobile phone.
He looks around furtively.*

BOHEMIAN: Um, oh good, um…

ROBBIE: (*Approaches.*) Hey! Jude Law! You got a pound?

*OMO lets go of BOHEMIAN. BOHEMIAN jumps up, seizing his
chance to escape from OMO.*

BOHEMIAN: Um, yes, here you go. (*Gives ROBBIE a coin and
dashes off.*)

ROBBIE: Oi! This is a penny, you stingy arse ham! (*To OMO.*)
You got a pound?

OMO: I don't have any money.

ROBBIE: Of course you don't, black man. More Rotary, less
roti! How long you going to rely on Live Aid, huh? All I'm
asking for is a lousy pound.

OMO: I wish I could help. Sorry.

ROBBIE: Stuff your sorry, yeah? I need to top up my mobile. I
got to spread the word. Something big is going down… I
said something big is going down.

OMO draws nearer.

Copped this off an MI5 agent while she was sliding down
chicken wings in Nando's.

OMO: You did?

ROBBIE: (*Yells.*) Fucking alert the cavalry!

OMO: Sorry. So you know a big secret.

ROBBIE: The biggest. I've unfolded the folded lie. (*Beckons
OMO to come closer. Conspiratorially.*) This government, yeah,
are you listening! Jeez… This government is plotting to
sterilize the Melanites.

OMO: The who?

ROBBIE: The thirteenth tribe of Judah. You. Me. Black people!

OMO: Oh, sorry. Is that true?

ROBBIE: Baby fathers are gonna make like 1066. We're gonna be history.

A cheer from all the nearby GIRLS.

(*Yells.*) You'd like that wouldn't you? Bitches.

GIRL 1: You ain't getting any, babe?

GIRL 2: He looks like a one minute man to me. That includes thirty seconds to take off his trousers.

GIRL 1: Shame! Shame!

They laugh.

ROBBIE: You want some? You want some?

GIRL 1: I'll give you some! (*Pulls out a knife.*)

ROBBIE hides behind OMO.

GIRL 2: Come on, babe. It's Robbie. He's a wanker.

GIRL 1: Your lucky day.

They exit.

ROBBIE: That's it, run.

OMO: You should take your information to the police.

ROBBIE: The police? Are you stupid?

OMO: Then go to the media.

ROBBIE: They're all involved! Didn't you see *Notting Hill?* That's the vision of a future Britain, man. It's all in here, in black and white. Long time man's been telling brothers about The Project for the New Anglo-Saxon Century.

OMO: And then what happens next?

ROBBIE: You really are stupid. Just like the rest of these sleepwalkers. (*Points around. Yells.*) They're coming for all of

you, yeah? Yeah! You too white trash! Don't think you're
safe. The Berkeley Plan is going to take care of you.

OMO: The Berkeley Plan?

ROBBIE: If you want to hide something from a black man, put
it in a book! Dickhead! Who's going to clean the streets
and drive the buses when we're gone? Bridewell Corp's
already signed the contract. Says so right here, man. (*Taps
the briefcase.*) Should have happened years ago but the
Prime Minister set back the timetable when he said we're
all middle-class.

OMO: He's called a halt to this project.

ROBBIE: For fuck's sake. *For fuck's sake.* He was off message. Big
business has smacked him on the wrist. Things are back on
track now. It's only a matter of time.

OMO: So how do we fight this plan?

ROBBIE: You got a bomb? What idiot question is that?

OMO: After the suffering, through peaceful means. If we rally
enough people…

ROBBIE: You shit: you're the establishment's foundation.
They're going to roast our balls!

OMO: We must go through fire before we raise the citadel.

ROBBIE: Let me tell you something, yeah. Peace is inbuilt into
the system to keep us down. Be grateful for your lot when
they feed you scraps. Be the bigger man when they shit on
you. Show dignity when the foot is on your neck. And we
buy into it wilfully. Peace my arse.

OMO: The wilful peace…

ROBBIE: Trickle down economy? More like tinkle down
economy. We're the ones getting pissed on.

OMO: The wilful peace…

ROBBIE: Call it what you like. The house always wins yet we keep playing their game.

OMO: The wilful peace…

ROBBIE: Yeah and you're part of it. I'm having none of that. I've opted out of society.

OMO: If you opt out who will tell the people the truth?

ROBBIE: Look around you! You think this lot want to wake up to face reality? Nah man, they can dream in their sleep. You open their eyes to realise they've got fuck-all that's too much information. Because then they have to do something about it. They can't pretend ignorance no more. They can't hide behind the god of that's-your-lot.

OMO: But what if I told you that I can help destroy the wilful peace?

ROBBIE: You ain't got a bomb.

OMO: I do not need one. I will gather the meek of Brixton in a union of souls. We shall all speak with one voice.

ROBBIE: You still riding that peace and love mule? Why not perform a miracle while you're at it.

OMO: A miracle is a sign, nothing else.

ROBBIE: Oh yeah? I'd like to see you convince these MOTHERFUCKING SHITHEADS how you're going to topple the ogre without waving your magic wand.

OMO: Belief is the key, and action soon follows. Believe.

ROBBIE: I believe in opting out. Steer clear of the establishment. That's action, man. That's me saying and doing. If you can't blow this place to kingdom come, yeah, keep your mouth shut. There's already too many talkers. Got to text my mates. They'll believe me now I got proof. You sure you haven't got a pound on you?

A WOMAN passes by, carrying a large number of newspapers. Sees ROBBIE.

WOMAN: Robbie Wedderburn! You still here? Giro office shuts in ten minutes.

ROBBIE: Shit! (*Jumps up.*) You don't have a pound on you, do you?

WOMAN: (*For the umpteenth time.*) No, Robbie. I don't have a pound.

ROBBIE dashes off. He leaves behind the briefcase.

He's read too many books. They ought to close down the library. It's a mental health hazard.

OMO: You read a lot yourself. (*Points to the papers.*)

WOMAN: I don't read them. I'm wise enough now. The price goes up tomorrow. I'll sell them at a profit.

OMO: (*Looks at the papers.*) But they're all today's.

WOMAN: (*Pause.*) That bastard newsagent!

OMO: (*Realises that MAN has forgotten his briefcase. He picks it up.*)Your friend forgot his briefcase. Will you keep it for him? He said there's secret information inside it.

WOMAN: Robbie's the biggest tall tale teller.

OMO: He sounded like he was telling the truth.

WOMAN: Sonny, never trust a man who's still on pay as you go.

OMO: He had such conviction. A man like that can move mountains.

WOMAN: I suppose you can make bread from clouds if you believe. Whether you can eat it is another matter.

OMO: Would you like to learn the truth?

WOMAN: (*Contemplates.*) Nah. I don't want to end up like Robbie. (*Exits. Off.*) Oi! Vendor!

OMO looks at the briefcase. Warily, he opens it. A DRUNK passes by.

DRUNK: All right?

OMO: (*Shuts the briefcase.*) I'm fine. And you?

DRUNK: Nothing like a can of Special Brew to make you feel special. (*Drinks.*) That's my working day over. Unless I can cadge a fag off you.

OMO: I don't smoke.

DRUNK: I don't smoke either but if you pushed me to the wall, dunked my head in water put a gun to my head, I'll inhale.

OMO: A question. What if I said I could help you overthrow the wilful peace that is holding you down?

DRUNK: (*Looks around, bewildered.*) No one's holding me down.

OMO: But what if I said I would no longer wait for the one crying in the wilderness, would you drop your can and follow me?

DRUNK: (*Looks at his can.*) It's either I'm plastered or you're chatting shit.

OMO: Would you change your life and follow me if I showed you proof?

DRUNK: Ah! Is it in there? (*Points to the briefcase.*) Come on, open it. There might be a ciggie in there you don't know about. Come on!

OMO is about to open the briefcase when the town hall bell rings.

Maria's on!

CITIZENS run excitedly across the stage, chanting:

CITIZENS: Maria's on, Maria's on.

OMO: Who is Maria?

DRUNK: Everybody knows Maria Maudlin, the Union Jack.

OMO: Is that her real name?

DRUNK: Who cares? (*Exits.*)

OMO: Maria Maudlin. Is she the one crying in the wilderness? (*Exits.*)

A WOMAN with a half-eaten chicken wing enters, frantic. She sees the briefcase and dashes to it. She checks the contents, sighs with relief and exits with it.

CITIZENS: (*As they set up the gentleman's club.*) Maria's on, Maria's on.

Music. A crucifix descends. MARIA MAUDLIN, in a Union Jack bikini, wrapped in the Union Jack, dances around a pole. Citizens become PUNTERS. They sway and groan to the music as they ogle her and hold their crotches. OMO looks at her squarely in the face. All freeze, except for MARIA who continues dancing, and OMO, who continues to stare at her.

MARIA: I hate the day shift. Too many prying eyes with empty wallets. My boss thought he'd hit the motherlode. Catch the giro junkies just after they pick up their cheques. Too bad, these Brixton boys aren't that desperate to hand over their money. Another of my boss's bright ideas was to convert this old church into a gentleman's club. Gentrification will bring in new money. Someone should have told him. The rich have their clubs where they worship their lucre. The poor just keep on coming. I hate this place. But I can't stop dancing.

Unfreeze.

PUNTER 1: Bada-Bing, Bada-Bong, Bada-Bang…

PUNTER 2: It's my first time here. Why is she called Union Jack?

PUNTER 3: Because she makes us ejaculate in unison.

ALL: (*Sigh.*) Ah… (*They hum 'God Save the Queen'.*)

OMO: Maria Maudlin… Maria Maudlin!

MARIA: My G-string's empty. Fill it up or shut up.

OMO: Maria Maudlin. I have come.

MARIA: Glad to help. Cheapskate.

OMO: Kiss my feet.

MARIA: Is that the new street for give me a blow-job?

PUNTERS shake their heads in unison.

OMO: Kiss my feet.

MARIA: Kiss my arse.

OMO: Kiss my feet.

MARIA: Fuck yourself.

OMO: Kiss my feet.

MARIA: Go to hell.

OMO: Maria Maudlin, know yourself. You are not a cunt. I will return.

MARIA: The bouncers will be waiting. Fuckwit.

PUNTERS: (*Jerk off.*) Ah…

MARIA: I'm on form. That was quick.

OMO: Paul was right. A prophet must make good abroad before his people recognise him. My Father will show me a sign among the Gentiles. I will gather my twelve and I will return in triumph to redeem the people of Brixton.

Soundscape: The music from the gentleman's club morphs into the sound of the underground. All that remains from the previous scene is the pole.

OMO, in the tube. PASSENGERS jammed up around the pole, some with their heads stuck in newspapers, magazines, novels. The rest hold on to the pole. They all avoid making eye contact with each other. Those reading newspapers or magazines shake them in unison. Those reading novels turn the page in unison.

PASSENGERS: (*To the sound of the train.*) 'Grin and bear it. Grin and bear it. Moan and Groan. Grin and bear it. Grin and bear it...'

The train grinds to a halt. PASSENGERS sway and halt in unison.

DRIVER: (*Over the PA.*) This is your driver speaking. Sorry for the delay. There is a signal failure at Victoria Station. We're being held here until further notice.

PASSENGERS groan collectively. They shake their newspapers and continue reading, avoiding making eye contact with each other.

OMO: (*To a PASSENGER.*) Acknowledge me.

PASSENGERS move one step round the pole.

(*To the next PASSENGER.*) Acknowledge me.

PASSENGERS move one step round the pole.

(*To the next PASSENGER.*) Acknowledge me.

PASSENGER: (*Scottish.*) And you are?

OMO: I am the one.

PASSENGER: Nice to meet you, the 'one'.

OMO: You are a Gentile?

PASSENGER: I'm Scottish.

OMO: You don't live in Brixton?

PASSENGER: I used to. I've just moved to Kilburn.

OMO: Nice area?

PASSENGER: It's all right. It's got enough Celts to make devolution feel like a good idea.

OMO: There is strength in the union.

Train jolts. The PASSENGERS jolt in unison.

PASSENGER: Oh aye, you must have heard that we and the English are of the same stock after all. It could be a good thing. Or not. You're not a *Sassenach*. Why do you care about the Union?

OMO: I am British. Return with me to Brixton. Be part of the new foundation that is being laid.

PASSENGER: If you're talking about buying property I missed the boat. I cannae afford to live in Brixton.

OMO: Ask.

PASSENGER: Sorry?

OMO: Ask. You shall receive that and more.

PASSENGER: I'm not religious.

OMO spreads out his arms.

Oh ask you? You're on the wrong train. Brixton is the other way.

OMO: Your faith is like a raindrop that refuses to fall in a downpour. You could end up in an ocean.

PASSENGER: Or I could end up in a wee puddle.

OMO: Shrug off your unbelief and follow me.

The train starts moving.

PASSENGER: I beg your pardon?

OMO: (*Holds PASSENGER's face.*) Don't beg: take.

PASSENGER: That's what I get for acting English. (*Pushes OMO's hands off.*)

OMO: Know yourself. Acknowledge me as your redeemer /

PASSENGER: Could you step back from me, please?

PASSENGER 2: That's the problem with jocks. They talk to anybody.

OMO: (*Advances, arms outstretched. In the voice of Reverend Williams.*) Touch the screen! Touch the screen and your wish will come true! Together we shall destroy the wilful peace and you shall toil uselessly no more...

PASSENGER presses the emergency alarm. The train shudders to a halt.

PASSENGERS: (*They swear.*)

Sound of Celestial Church prayers. A baby crying.

Soundscape: The sound of the underground morphs into the sound of Brixton High Street.

A station assistant escorts OMO from Brixton station.

ASSISTANT: You understand what I told you? You're banned from the underground. (*Under his breath.*) Nutter.

OMO: The outside world rejects me. The concerns of the flesh prevail in the hearts of the fallen everywhere. (*Looks heavenwards.*) Now I understand why your people emphasize unconditional love. But that's fine with me. A father should be selfless for his children. Love establishes the link of blood. I'll have less work to do. Lastborns get it easy. You've shown me that the work must start here. First Brixton and then the world.

MARIA MAUDLIN passes by with shopping bags.

OMO: Maria Maudlin!

MARIA: Oh. It's you.

OMO: You will acknowledge me.

MARIA: Are you stalking me?

OMO: Maria Maudlin, there is work to be done. Together we will shake off the wilful peace. We will break the cycle of pain.

MARIA: This lady's doing just fine with the way things are. Stop following me.

OMO: I cannot break the cycle without you, Mother of the End Times.

MARIA: Too bad. I'm not the mother type.

OMO: Look into my eyes.

MARIA: They're beautiful, I know.

OMO: I see into your soul. It is full of beauty and light.

MARIA: I don't know who you think you are but...

OMO: You know who I am /

MARIA: Honestly I don't. OK? Now I'd love to stay and chat but I've got work to do.

OMO: The real work will begin. Soon we shall cross the river hand in hand and we shall shake off the wilful peace. Become, Maria. Become!

MARIA: You look like a nice guy. My advice, get a job and settle down. That's all there is to a happy life. No one's buying the new world you're peddling. (*Brings out a few coins.*) Here, buy yourself something to eat. And don't come looking for me any more.

The town hall bell rings.

OMO: You *are* the Mother! Alfie!

MARIA: Alfie the town crier? Alfie's dead. (*She exits.*)

Soundscape: Market noises.

DONA and OMO in Brixton Market. DONA is talking to a prospective convert, CITIZEN. OMO looks on but he is not paying attention. He holds a file and pen.

DONA: ...That's where you're wrong. God doesn't want me to wear sackcloth and live in dignified penury. He wants me to have the best things in life. Because this world and everything in it belongs to him, and we his children are his inheritors.

CITIZEN: So there's no catch? No charges, like inheritance tax?

DONA: (*Laughs.*) The Father's gifts are unconditional. He does not give with one hand and take with the other.

CITIZEN: So what do I have to do to buy into this scheme?

DONA: You don't have to buy into any scheme. All you have to do is give your life to the Lord, nothing else.

CITIZEN: Yeah but I still don't see how I'm going to pay off my mortgage. And thanks to the Olympics, God knows how much the surcharge on council tax will be /

DONA: All these worries mean nothing when you put your faith in the right place. As you are now the rat race is all you live for and it's leading you to run round in circles.

CITIZEN: (*Pauses, trying to make up his mind.*) You say you're from The Mission, right? You were in the news. You're supposed to be a cult.

DONA: The media are the world's biggest junk mailers. Don't believe what you read in the papers. Believe this: seventy per cent of our members are homeowners. Sixty per cent of us have our children in private schools. Forty per cent of us are debt-free.

CITIZEN: Hm, sounds phenomenal.

DONA: Phenomenal it is, Brother. If I can just take your name... Brother Omo... *Brother Omo.*

OMO wakes up from his reverie and hands DONA the file and pen.

(*Hands CITIZEN the file.*) Here you go...

CITIZEN writes down his name. Hands DONA back the file.

See you in church on Sunday.

CITIZEN leaves.

Brother Omo. You're making me regret that I chose you as my partner. So many other missionaries wanted this patch. I stood up for you.

OMO: I'm sorry. My mind wandered. I understand the Good News approach as a way of finding the Lord.

DONA: Good. That's excellent. So what's bothering you now?

OMO: (*Hesitates.*) First you were luring the vulnerable.

DONA: Excuse me: I was not luring the vulnerable. They're the ones who need to hear the good news the most. I thought you understood…

OMO: Now you're attracting the new money, those who are gentrifying Brixton.

DONA: How do you think we raise money for the prisoners programme? If not for our high income members giving generously we would not have met and you would not have been saved.

OMO: Our Father willed that I should be saved through you.

DONA: Exactly but we live in the world. Our Father knows that and he rewards us in the world. If you calculate Abraham's net worth in today's terms, Bill Gates couldn't touch him.

OMO: And the rewards that the Father gives us are different.

DONA: Each according to their desires. To he who has even more shall be added.

OMO: Meaning the rich get richer the poor get poorer and must beg charity from the rich?

DONA: The poor will always be here with us. This is the only way we can help them.

OMO: By making gods of the rich.

DONA: He's not rich… Let's find a quiet corner.

They move to one side of the stage. CITIZENS OF BRIXTON, those left behind, engage in a heated argument over a parcel. They glare at DONA and OMO. DONA and OMO move to the opposite side of the stage.

(*Holds OMO's hands.*) Brother Omo, I know all the troubles you've been through. You're trying to find order in your life and that's fine. The Mission provides that for us. It's pointless you questioning everyone and everything. You'll only get confused. You must submit yourself to us to direct you. Jesus said we must be like children.

OMO: Children always ask questions.

DONA: And you know how annoying that is. You cannot function if you keep muddying the water. Life is simple. Don't overload it with unnecessary complications. You want to change the world? That's not our job.

OMO: Then whose job is it?

DONA: God's. And until He creates a different kind of human being that change you're hankering after is a pipe dream. (*Pause.*) Go home, have a lie down. I'll come by later and we'll pray together, all right? (*She squeezes his arm affectionately.*) Go. (*She sees GREG, walking by with camcorder.*) Brother, have you heard the good news?

GREG ignores her and passes by. She tries to go after him but backtracks when he stands by the CITIZENS and focuses his camcorder on them. He gets too close to the CITIZENS and gets entangled with them. He shields his camcorder from damage. He gets shoved to one side as the CITIZENS become more aggressive with each other.

The HOMELESS WOMAN enters. She sees DONA and backtracks. DONA sees her.

Sister! Sister! You promised me you'd come to service…
(*Exits after WOMAN.*)

OMO: (*Restless.*) Change. Transform the world. Unfold the folded lie. The time has surely come. (*Looks heavenwards.*) Show me the sign. (*He exits.*)

GREG adjusts his camcorder and films the CITIZENS OF BRIXTON *who start fighting over the parcel. The parcel comes apart, releasing white powder into the air. The* CITIZENS *inhale. They dance with each other, singing 'Make Peace, Not War'.*

Police siren. A gunshot. All freeze, except for GREG.

GREG: I've been here for how long and I still don't have an original angle. I mean, how does one inscribe Brixton without the usual signposts of drugs, violence and the shining white knight called gentrification? What strategies can I employ to 'de-exoticise' the natives? I've called it the Brixton challenge. My mates in the studio call me Don Quixote. 'You didn't want this gig and now you're trying to make things harder for yourself.' To be honest, it's hard work trying to see the world any other way except through the grand narrative bestowed on us...them...from up above. The hardest way up the mountain is by taking the route less travelled. And from where I'm standing, my friends in high places seem even further away. (*Pauses.*) Fuck it. I'm calibrating my lens to normal focus. Let some other mug search for the real Brixton. To be honest, what would I gain from humanising these beasts of England? They're wild life, primetime fodder. And I shall serve them to you in a tale of the expected, just as you want it. Go with the flow, on with the show. The already written formula guarantees box office success. (*GREG films the* CITIZENS.) Get past this blip and move on to better things. Come on you morons, fight! (*Disappointed, he puts down his camcorder. He stays where he is.*)

Police siren starts again.

The CITIZENS OF BRIXTON *unfreeze. Quickly, they set up the gentleman's club and become the* PUNTERS. *The* PUNTERS *jerk off to* MARIA *dancing around the pole.*

PUNTER: Bada-Bing, Bada-Bong, Bada-Bang…

PUNTERS: (*Sing.*) 'Maria Maudlin, Maria Maudlin, Maria
Maudlin…'

GREG: 'Maria Maudlin.' Is that your real name?

MARIA: Who wants to know?

GREG: My name's Greg. I'm a journalist. I want to do a feature
on you.

MARIA: You want to do a number on me.

GREG: Feature. I said feature.

MARIA: I heard you right the first time, sonny. Thanks but no
thanks.

GREG: It's a piece on Brixton but I'll make you the
centrepiece. What do you say? Have Middle Englanders
wet themselves over you?

MARIA: You heard me right the first time.

GREG: I could make you the angel of Brixton.

MARIA: You missed me by a lifetime. This angel's face is way
too dirty now.

GREG: Get a face wipe and join the queue. How did you
become a pole dancer?

MARIA: Don't ask me stupid questions.

GREG: Stupid questions get the truth.

MARIA: The truth or the answers you want?

GREG: Same thing.

MARIA: In your book. The way you look at me through that
camera. The contempt sandblasted onto your face. Is that
your SW4 sneer?

GREG: I look this way all the time.

MARIA: You're a shit stirrer. You're a voyeur.

GREG: One or the other. A little of both. Hey, I'm a journalist. I like you. You make good copy.

MARIA: That's made my day. Now take your box of tricks and go play in someone else's garden.

GREG: You're turning down an opportunity to change your life.

MARIA ignores him. GREG focuses his camcorder on MARIA. PUNTERS stand up to him.

(*Continues filming them.*) Scowl for the camera, boys. Show me that urban grittiness.

PUNTERS adopt gangsta poses.

That's what I want. You: move one step to the left. You're blocking Maria.

PUNTERS take their used tissues and smear GREG and his camcorder with it.

Ah fuck!

PUNTERS laugh and return to their seats.

You fucking wankers! (*Brings out a handkerchief. Cleans himself.*)

GREG cursing retreats, bumping into OMO. He glares at OMO. OMO smiles at him.

GREG exits.

MARIA: (*Sees OMO.*) Oh for God's sake!

OMO: (*Looks her in the eyes.*) Maria Maudlin I have come.

MARIA: If you're going to be a regular you can at least follow the etiquette: unzip your flies and zip your mouth.

OMO: Maria Maudlin, acknowledge me.

MARIA: Haven't you got your work to do? Shake off the wilful whatever.

OMO: Maria Maudlin did you attend Oxford?

MARIA: Is today Stupid Questions Day? I'm a pole-dancing prostitute. What do you think?

OMO: You are the foundation of the wilful peace.

CITIZENS: Matriculate, graduate, ejaculate. Ah!

OMO: (*Points to CITIZENS.*) You lock them in the cycle. You prevent them from unfolding the folded lie.

MARIA: And how do my origami skills stop you from getting a job?

OMO: The scales will fall from your eyes. You will be my angel.

MARIA: That's twice in one day I've been called an angel. Hate to spoil your fantasy but this angel is a cunt.

OMO: Every harlot was a virgin once.

MARIA: No one can live with their fantasy. Reality gets in the way.

OMO: (*Climbs onto the table. Looks her straight in the eye.*) Maria Maudlin, you are my reality.

MARIA: I can't stop dancing.

OMO: Then I shall dance with you.

They dance together. OMO traps MARIA with his eyes. They slide to the floor, wrapped in the Union Jack. The PUNTERS whoop and catcall.

Tate Gardens, in front of Brixton Library. CITIZEN 2 enters, singing. He has a great voice.

CITIZEN 2: I'm gonna get paid
I'm gonna get paid
I'm gonna get paid
And after, get laid.

CITIZEN 1 enters. He wears African beads around his neck.

CITIZEN 1: How you doing, man?

CITIZEN 2: What's with the beads? Don't tell me you've joined another cult.

CITIZEN 1: Afrocentrism is not a cult, Brother.

CITIZEN 2: How long this time?

CITIZEN 1: This is the one for me, unbeliever. I'm returning to the source. I'm black, and that's a fact.

CITIZEN 2: So what, you gonna call yourself some name I can't pronounce?

CITIZEN 1: You'd better start learning, African. From now on I'm Oladipupo Olugbolahan Titilola Olatunde. How does that sound?

CITIZEN 2: Like you threw up a scrabble board. What's wrong with Cuthbert?

CITIZEN 1: That was my slave name and a noncey one too.

CITIZEN 2: You been listening to 'acknowledge me' guy again? He's a Christian you idiot. More to the point, he's off his head.

CITIZEN 1: Maybe he's from Bahia. They mix Christianity with Orisha.

CITIZEN 2: He ain't from Bahia.

CITIZEN 1: How do you know?

CITIZEN 2: Does he sound Brazilian to you? By tomorrow you're gonna tell me you're Moslem.

CITIZEN 1: But what if, just for the sake of argument that Omo's the real deal? If he could grant you one wish, what would you wish for?

CITIZEN 2: You know I don't believe in that shit.

CITIZEN 1: Humour me.

CITIZEN 2: Only one wish? Man, that's stingy. Genies grant three wishes.

CITIZEN 1: Yeah, it's all the funding cuts, innit? So?

CITIZEN 2: Let's see – one wish… I would wish for an end to world hunger and I'd wish for world peace.

CITIZEN 1: What are you, Miss World? And I said *one* wish.

CITIZEN 2: It's the same thing. No hunger – world peace.

CITIZEN 1: You're too poor to be a liberal.

CITIZEN 2: One wish yeah? OK, I'd wish for land reform. No one can own land, not even forty acres. You can be the Duke of Dukesberry or the Bum of Bumsville. Land reform equals equality equals peace. There.

CITIZEN 1: You're a dreamer.

CITIZEN 2: If this guy was the messiah then I'd be in his good books, see. He'd put me in his cabinet and then I could have anything I want. Smart, eh? What would you wish for?

CITIZEN 1: I'd wish to be white.

CITIZEN 2: For real?

CITIZEN 1: Yup.

CITIZEN 2: You serious?

CITIZEN 1: With the bluest eyes.

CITIZEN 2: Man, you shook off your Afrocentrism quick time.

CITIZEN 1: Black people ain't even kings in Africa. All those queens got their head-wraps on too tight, they are gonna be in for a shock when they get to the pearly gates.

CITIZEN 2: What, so God's a racist?

CITIZEN 1: None of the disciples was called Amantutanerfertiti.

CITIZEN 2: Oh come on!

CITIZEN 1: Don't matter how many times you attend service or sleep with the vicar, we're pre-fabbed for keeping hellfire burning.

CITIZEN 2: You're so full of shit.

CITIZEN 1: The truth is hard, bro'. Coal fire for hell. That's us. At hell's gate there's this giant with a shovel throwing us into the oven. Cos that's all we're good for in the white man's faith. We can't even get into hell. You can sing so you might have a chance. Lefties don't know it but Thatcher did white people a favour when she closed the mines.

CITIZEN 2: What!

CITIZEN 1: Them miners that were getting killed down below, they were being mistaken for brothers when they crossed over. That was the only time God broke his covenant with white people.

CITIZEN 2: Nah, nah, you gone too far now.

CITIZEN 1: Oh yeah? Where did the term, 'to welsh on an agreement' come from then?

CITIZEN 2: I'm telling all the guys you want to be white.

CITIZEN 1: I knew you'd fall for it!

CITIZEN 2: Yes 'cos you're not joking.

CITIZEN 1: Now why would I want to be white?

CITIZEN 2: Tell that to the guys.

CITIZEN 1: I was winding you up. I'm glad I'm black.

CITIZEN 2: You'd better be.

CITIZEN 1: For real. But let's be honest. Equal opportunities hasn't reached the church and I ain't sure it's reached the Great Upstairs. On earth as it is in heaven, man. There ain't no black messiah in my Bible. Better we go with the black man's god. Edumare ain't gonna mistake me for coal.

SARAH enters with shopping. Her shopping bag falls from her lap. She struggles to pick up the fallen items. OMO enters. He helps her.

SARAH: Thanks. Dona let you off her leash for today?

OMO: Do I look like a prisoner to you, Sarah Green?

SARAH: You look like someone who could be doing something more useful than standing round Coldharbour Lane getting on everyone's nerves, don't you think?

OMO: Do you know that you are good for so much more, Sarah Green?

SARAH: Oh I've been good all right. Good for lots more than you could ever imagine. Don't you know who I am?

OMO: Do you know who I am?

SARAH: Oh you're some kind of seer. What are you doing with Dona and her people?

OMO: What were you looking for with them?

SARAH: You really must have Nigerian roots. You answer a question with a question. (*Wheels off.*) I've got to see my therapist.

OMO: If you only believe.

SARAH: (*Stops.*) I was chockablock with belief. Look at me now.

OMO: You have tried and you have failed on your own.

SARAH: You really don't remember me. How could you say that I'm a failure?

OMO: I mean in your search for a new you /

SARAH: The 'English Rose'. You've forgotten me so soon? You watched me on TV running the hundred metres for Great Britain, winning Olympic gold, draped in the Union Jack. You remember me, don't you? You called me, you called me 'Our Sarah'. *Our Sarah.* I thought: this is only the beginning. I'm going onto glory representing my country. I put Brixton on the world map. I was going to be a role model for urban youths. Life was going to be one long cruise. I am the English Rose, I can never wilt. Then I woke up one morning, my legs were gone. And I cried. I cried so hard my pupils turned red. I asked every god known to man, why me? I marched against the war. I bought the wristband. I take photos with children. The driver said he didn't see me. Yet he testified that I didn't look before I stepped onto the road...

OMO: You can be the flag bearer of this nation again. You can help raise the people so that their day of glory will not pass them. The people and their children will live to see the dawn of a New Jerusalem. Join me.

SARAH: Tell Dona I'm never coming back. I don't appreciate being made a fool of.

OMO: I do not understand.

SARAH: I'm a person. I'm not some icon you can use as a marketing tool for your church.

OMO: I am not talking on Dona's behalf.

SARAH: First that prostitute uses my image for the entertainment of those dogs. Then you people. This is how you treat a sister when she's down? (*Wheels off.*)

OMO: Sarah! (*He goes after her.*)

CITIZENS 1 and 2 call to him.

CITIZEN 1: Brother Omo! Say the word.

OMO: (*He stops.*) You would like to hear the word?

CITIZEN 2: We're going nowhere.

OMO: Acknowledge me.

CITIZEN 2: Sure, we acknowledge you.

CITIZEN 1: Yep, you're you.

OMO: (*Looks after SARAH. Shows them his pendant.*) The stone of
Brihtsige: Brixton to you. Anonymous masses, incredible
mavericks: indistinguishable, yet each one of you unique.
I am the builder. You are the blocks of the New Jerusalem.
Every step draws us closer to the crossing of the river for
the overthrow of the wilful peace. I am the one you prayed
would come and revoke your life sentence of second-class
citizenship, the one who will smash the cycle of pain. You
must transform yourselves, now when it is time for the
meek to inherit the nation. Come out of your Otherness.
Like a butterfly breaking out of its chrysalis, reveal your
true selves. Revel in your own reflection. Belief, that's all
you need. The middle passage, the criss-cross of Atlantic
journeys that brought us to these shores bursting with
meanings yet to be explained. Let the nightmare become
the dream. The touch of a finger and monuments crumble.
And yet we have let the wilful peace reign. Through *détente*,
compromise, complacency. Here is the front line. Cross
it and be transformed into a new being with new passions
screaming for breath. Release yourselves of your double
consciousness. Come and be renewed in the oneness of
being. Come and be born anew.

Drumbeat. OMO *performs the Dance of the Washing, waving
the handkerchief.*

Mirror me and with elation unbridled, fondle your most
lurid memories. Then let go! Smash the cycle of pain. Now
with fear discarded cross over! (*Dances.*) Go forth, go forth!

*CITIZENS sway uncomfortably, trying to copy OMO. They end up
doing a kind of Morris dance.*

CITIZEN 1: I thought he said go forth. He's surrendering. Can
we cut out the dance?

CITIZEN 2: Bruv! Who are you again?

DONA enters.

OMO: I am the one you prayed would come. I am here and I
will never leave you. I will never die. Lastborns get it easy.

CITIZEN 1: Speak for yourself. I'm a lastborn and all I got was this lousy tee-shirt.

CITIZEN 1 and CITIZEN 2 laugh and high-five each other.

CITIZEN 2: Stop speaking in parables, man. Who are you?

CITIZEN 1: Who are you?

CITIZEN 2: Who are you?

ALL: (*À la football chant:*) 'Who-are-yer, who-are yer, who-are-yer?'...

OMO: I am the son of /

DONA: Brother Omo! (*To the CITIZENS.*) He's sick, please excuse him. There's nothing more to see. Go!

CITIZENS drift away.

What do you think you're doing?

OMO: They acknowledged me.

DONA: They acknowledged nothing. You are embarrassing The Mission. You cannot go round inferring, inferring that you're the messiah. You are Omo, do you hear me?

OMO: They acknowledged me.

DONA: We'll go see Dr Gupta. He'll put you back on medication. Until then, I don't want you out preaching. You will stay in the bed-sit until I see that you are suitably recovered.

OMO: Anger has a certain beauty, just before it tips over into rage. You're borderline.

DONA: (*Struggles to control herself.*) I am not angry, Brother Omo. I am disappointed in you.

OMO: Don't be. I haven't started the work /

DONA: Don't say another word. I'll fix an appointment with the clinic for tomorrow. I have to run an errand.

OMO: When will you stop running for The Mission and attend to your soul?

DONA: When I become a minister I will help raise the souls of thousands. I'll be able to heal you completely of your sickness. But right now, do not let The Mission hear about this.

OMO: For my sake or for yours, Dona?

Citizens of Brixton set up OMO's bed-sit. MARIA MAUDLIN lies on the bed.

You are blinded by your craving to scale The Mission's hierarchy.

DONA: I have asked you to go home.

OMO: Asked or ordered?

DONA: Don't bite the hand that raised you out of bondage.

They stare at each other. DONA exits. OMO takes off his top.

The following day.

The bed-sit. MARIA is in bed sleeping. OMO is looking through the DVDs.

MARIA stirs from the bed.

MARIA: What time is it?

OMO: I didn't mean to wake you. Sorry.

MARIA: What time's Dona coming?

OMO: The people, they didn't really believe me.

MARIA: Don't let that get you down.

OMO: They say they need a leader yet they refuse to answer my call.

MARIA: You're only a spectacle they use to pass the time with, the latest crank claiming to be God. And the white hanky. What was that all about?

OMO: It's a sign of victory.

MARIA: In Africa, maybe. You know here it means surrender.

OMO: It's a sign of peace, love and eternal victory.

MARIA: It means different if you keep acting weird.

OMO stretches out his arms and yawns.

Yeah, you see – that Christ complex: I'm not feeling it. Why didn't you say you're Lobsang Rampa or Mother Teresa?

OMO: Become the sign, Maria. Reveal the divine revelation to me.

MARIA: You've read too much into *The Da Vinci Code.* I'll tell you who I am. I'm a woman who's been down on her luck as many times as I've gone down on men. I can't remember how many times I've had to check into bad luck rehab. I've been Maria Maudlin for so long I can't remember if I ever had another name. But I'm alive. And I'm right here. In the end that's all that counts because I can bear witness that my luck can change. I've snagged my 'messiah'.

OMO: I am serious Maria. (*He sits beside her.*)

MARIA: So am I.

OMO: Have you had many men?

MARIA: What a question to ask a lady! Ah well, you could have been downright rude and asked me my age.

OMO: It makes no difference about how I feel about you. I see you for who you are and I love you.

MARIA: I've had enough men to turn me into the strong black woman. When I looked into your eyes I knew. You looked right into my soul. You wanted *me*.

OMO: In you I find purity. I find the beating heart that will rock the foundations of the establishment.

MARIA: It's fun you trying to be special. I can tell you, it's the kind of party you should leave early. After a while you begin to get bored. You start to wish to be like every other Joe. And before you know it time has passed and you realise all the things you have are not the things you really wanted. You start to think if I get another chance, I'd rewrite that script.

OMO: I have to fulfil my mission.

MARIA: It's a mission that you've been crap at so far. Give the people their miracle. They won't follow you just because you talk a good talk, not Brixtonians. Give them their fifteen minutes of belief and let them go look for the next prophet to sell them hope. (*She wraps her arms round him.*) The world's a turbulent place if you don't have an anchor.

OMO: My Father is my anchor.

MARIA: Oh.

OMO: He is the only one who can be called good.

MARIA: He's still living?

OMO: He was with me all the time I was in prison.

MARIA: He came to see you everyday?

OMO: He reminded me that I am His son.

MARIA: How come I've never seen him? You don't want him to know about me?

OMO: I can never be ashamed of you, Maria. Believe me, neither is my Father. Oh He has seen you Maria, and He says you are the most beautiful creature on earth. He is pleased with you.

MARIA: Oh. You mean... (*She points upwards.*) Yeah.

The alarm clock rings.

OMO: Don't go. Stay with me.

MARIA: The day you get a job is the last day I'll be Maria Maudlin. (*Takes a pill from her handbag.*) Force of habit. Just in case this is all too good to be true.

OMO: You do not need that, Maria.

MARIA: It's all right.

OMO: (*Takes her hand which holds the pill. Looks straight into her eyes.*) You do not need that. Trust me. All your pain belongs in the past. We are one, Maria. (*Drops the pill and crushes it underfoot.*)

The town hall clock bell rings.

Alfie!

MARIA: Don't! When I said I wanted you to be you I meant whatever you are underneath this mirage you project. I'm as close as I can be to you and still you're not letting me in.

OMO: I am, Maria. You refuse to see me as I am.

MARIA: Suit yourself. (*Turns away.*) Miss Watchtower will soon be here. (*Dresses.*) I have time for a coffee. Make me a mug.

OMO: Don't fear about the new course your life will take.

MARIA: Forget about the coffee. Hand me my blouse.

OMO: (*Holds MARIA.*) Do you believe that I am who I say I am?

MARIA: You haven't heard a word I said.

OMO: Do you love me?

MARIA: Not in the way you want me to. I can't measure up to whatever ideal you've got in your head.

OMO: Say yes you believe me. Then say yes you love me. That's all I ask.

DONA enters.

DONA: Brother Omo, sorry about yesterday. I didn't want to leave you…

Pause.

You have nothing to say for yourself? The Mission is washing its hands of you. You have a week's notice to vacate the flat. (*She makes to exit. She turns back.*) How does it feel, fornicating with a 'messiah'? What's it like playing a part in his sick pantomime /

MARIA: Watch your mouth, choir girl.

DONA: He hasn't a clue who his parents are. They took one look at him and they dumped him in a bin on Coldharbour Lane. Did he tell you he went to prison for impersonating people? Not identity theft to defraud them. He stole their lives because he's got no family to call his own. (*To OMO.*) Because God's family isn't good enough for you! And I humoured you. I thought living here would help you to settle down and move on with your life. The Mission took you in. I took you in and this is how you show me your gratitude.

MARIA puts on her coat.

OMO: Maria…

MARIA opens her handbag and takes out a pill. She swallows it and exits.

Maria…

DONA: You're out of here by week end.

OMO heads after MARIA. DONA blocks his way. She holds out her hand. OMO hands her the crucifix. He grabs the nearest top, his caftan, and exits.

DONA beckons to the CITIZENS. They enter and remove the set.

SARAH wheels by. GREG crosses by with his camcorder. He focuses on SARAH.

SARAH: Get that camcorder out of my face.

GREG: I know you. You're Sarah Green.

SARAH: You deaf?

GREG: (*Lowers the camcorder.*) Disability is the new black. You could win the sympathy vote on *I'm a Celebrity*. Make some money out of your tragedy.

SARAH glares at him.

Sorry to disturb you, 'English Rose'. (*Exits.*)

MARIA MAUDLIN enters, distraught. SARAH sees her.

SARAH: Hey! Maudlin!

MARIA passes SARAH by, ignoring her.

Don't ignore me!

MARIA: (*Turns round.*) What is it now?

SARAH: Stop desecrating my image!

MARIA: You don't own the rights to the flag.

SARAH: You had to copy me, imitate my pose. You had to turn my crowning moment into a cheap freak show.

MARIA: It's a bit of fun. If you'd been parodied on *Little Britain* you'd be whooping it up, blackface and all.

SARAH: How many more punters can that calcified cunt of yours take?

MARIA: I don't have time for this. My head is in a weird place.

SARAH: Because it's not down in some man's groin.

MARIA: I walked into that one.

SARAH: You can walk. I pass by you in this wheelchair every day yet you continue mocking me in that house of filth. What does that say about you as a person?

MARIA: You know I genuinely felt for you. A Brixton girl makes good and then this happens to you. But life doesn't stop just because you meet with tragedy, even for you, English Rose.

SARAH: Don't call me that you pus pit.

MARIA: That driver who knocked you down, he's going to hell. He let you live.

SARAH rams MARIA with her wheelchair. She boxes MARIA into a corner and continues ramming her. MARIA slaps her until she backs away. They glare at each other. A crowd gathers. OMO enters.

OMO: Maria! Maria…

MARIA: Don't touch me. (*Makes to leave.*)

OMO: I love you.

MARIA: I hate you.

OMO: Maria…

MARIA: Get a life! Get a life!

OMO: Maria!

A bell rings.

Alfie? It is time. Surely it is time. (*To the crowd, desperately.*) You have asked for a miracle, a sign to take for a wonder.

CITIZEN 1: Come on then! The bookies close in an hour.

OMO grabs SARAH's wheelchair. He pins her shoulders.

SARAH: (*Struggles with him.*) Let go of me! Let go!

OMO: Drink with me of the communion of blood that has been denied you since the crossing of the middle passage. Shake from your wrists the chains of double consciousness. Arise from your deathbed and become whole again. (*He brings out two handkerchiefs.*)

CITIZEN 1: Shit, not the handkerchief again.

SARAH: Keep your dirty hands off!

CITIZEN 2: Just perform a miracle, for God's sake! That's what Jesus would do.

CITIZEN 1: Not the dance. Please not the dance.

OMO sways.

Oh fuck.

OMO: Know the truth and it shall set you free! Independence is cure and poison. Only the truth can demolish the old foundation. Only then will you become truly manumitted in spirit and in body. Only then can we become a union of souls. Wave the handkerchief of freedom. Wave!

SARAH: Get off me you madman! Help! Help!

CITIZENS grudgingly wave their handkerchiefs. Slowly, SARAH stops struggling. CITIZENS notice this and start to wave with intent. OMO hands each end of his handkerchiefs to SARAH. SARAH takes them.

OMO: We are waves that will flood the institutions whose buildings grope the sky. We will drown the folded lie. The time has come for the leap across the river! For the river to flow with blood.

CITIZEN 2: Christ! He's fucking Enoch Powell returned as a black man. There is a God after all.

CITIZEN 1: (*Falls to his knees.*) God, make me white! Make me white!

CITIZEN 2 glares at him. CITIZEN 1 stands up sheepishly.

OMO: Now is the time, Father. Do not forsake me in my appointed hour. To you, Sarah Green I say: get up and walk!

OMO pulls on the handkerchiefs. Slowly, during his speech, SARAH rises up.

Break free of the cycle. Throw away your crutches. Claim your birthright of freedom. Believe! Believe.

The stage is covered in white light. CITIZENS *cower and shield their eyes. The light fades.* SARAH *is standing. She takes a tentative step, then another and then another.*

Uproar. CITIZENS *wave their handkerchiefs furiously.* MARIA *looks on in shock.*

SARAH *runs round the stage and exits.*

OMO: (*Dances, enraptured.*) Yes, Father! Yes, yes, yes!

The town hall bell rings crazily. CITIZENS *dance with* OMO, *waving their handkerchiefs. They exit together, leaving* MARIA MAUDLIN *stunned.*

SARAH *runs around the stage. She comes to centre-stage and jogs on the spot.*

SARAH: I can't stop running. I've run up and down Coldharbour Lane and up Brixton Hill. I'm on my second run round. I'm not tired. I've beaten my personal best by seconds. I feel as invincible as the day I took that gold medal. The English Rose is back and she smells twice as nice. (*She runs off.*)

DONA, *outside Brixton Station.*

DONA: (*Looks at her watch to see if it's still working. She looks up to the town hall clock.*) Ring, for goodness' sake!

People rush past her.

Brother, hear the good news! …Sister, receive the word! Where is everyone rushing to?

GREG *dashes in with a camcorder. He approaches* DONA.

GREG: (*Sees* DONA.) Where is he?

DONA: Who are you talking about?

GREG: Your friend, brother, co-conspirator. I saw you together. Omo or whatever his name is.

DONA: Omo is no longer with The Mission.

GREG: Come now. I know what you and your cult are up to.

DONA: The Mission is not a cult!

GREG: What is it, not raking enough from the collection plate?

DONA: I've had enough of you people smearing us.

GREG: Is that what your lot call the truth these days? I'll find out how you tricked the Brixtonites. I'll find out and I'll expose all of you for the power-lusting charlatans you are.

DONA slaps GREG.

Wow! If you think I'm just going to turn the other cheek /

DONA slaps him on the other cheek. GREG legs it. DONA rages after him.

From the other side of the stage, OMO enters, followed by the people of Brixton. He stands centre-stage. They surround him. His caftan is dirty. GREG dashes in with DONA hot on his tail. They stop to take in the scene. GREG records the event on his camcorder.

CITIZEN 1: Omo, please, it's my little boy's schooling. He's not in the right catchment area. I need to buy a house in Dulwich.

CITIZEN 2: The supermarkets are squeezing my margins. I've got a wife and kids to support. I just need to break even and to have spare.

CITIZEN 3: My hip operation's been postponed again. You don't have a waiting list for your miracles, do you?

CITIZEN 4: I promised the council I'd keep the noise down but they still want to kick me out of my flat.

CITIZEN 5: I swear I'll stop dealing on the high street. A hundred thousand pounds will do me.

CITIZEN 6: If you give me the lottery numbers for Saturday, I'll give ten per cent to your church. Make it ten and a half per cent.

OMO: This is not what I'm about.

CITIZEN 5: You're about transforming lives, innit? That's what we want too.

ALL: Yeah! Yeah!

GREG gets closer in expectation.

OMO: Abandon the wilful peace.

CITIZEN 6: Wipe clean the slate, topple the state, yeah? Well to me that sounds suicidal. Why d'you want to put your life in danger?

CITIZEN 3: Yeah. You're still black, you know. You ain't getting crucified for nobody. Just be the god of small things, man.

CITIZEN 6: This is our time.

ALL: Yeah! Yeah!

OMO: If you reject my message you deny my Father who has sent me.

CITIZEN 4: Yeah, well, never as good as the first time, innit?

CITIZEN 3: You mad?

CITIZEN 4: I'm just saying, man.

OMO: You are satisfied to be the footnote in the grand narrative of others. Has it come that the crumbs from the master's table to you are now a buffet? Now when I offer you the chance to become the acknowledged legislators of your destinies, to shape the world in your own image, you withdraw to the lines of *détente*? You have received the hammer and you now pretend that you cannot see the nail? For how long will you be the consumers of your woes? For how long do you choose to remain beasts of England?

CITIZEN 5: Hey! We're not asking for too much. Ask your man Jesus if he really wanted to have his arse nailed to a cross.

CITIZEN 6: That's right! You ain't the final curtain. I never heard you warning about the End Times.

CITIZEN 5: Thank you! Not even a parable.

CITIZEN 6: There you go. So, please, no revolution. A good life in this world, that's all we want.

ALL: Yeah! Yeah!

CITIZEN 3: And rims! I want rims!

CITIZEN 4: The good life for us all in this country. That's what I'd call a revolution. Is that too hard for you to give us?

OMO looks at the CITIZENS. He shakes his head as he makes to depart.

CITIZEN 3: Omo where are you going? Omo!

CITIZEN 4: Truly it is written in *The Mail,* 'Can anything good come out of Brixton?'

The CITIZENS surround him, blocking his way, begging him not to leave.

DONA: Don't beg him! He's a fake! How did you get these people to believe in your heresy?

CITIZEN 5: It's not hearsay. I saw it with my own eyes.

DONA: Renounce yourself now!

GREG goes closer to her. She shoves him away.

Where is she? Where is Maria Maudlin?

CITIZENS: (*Dreamily.*) Ah...

One of the CITIZENS smiles sheepishly. He has wet himself.

DONA: You and that harlot are in collusion. You've duped these poor fools. You will rot in hell right next to her.

CITIZEN 3: Sister. It was not Maria Maudlin.

CITIZEN 4: Yeah, it was the wheelchair woman. Hyacinth Bucket what's her face?

DONA: Sarah? Sarah Green?

CITIZEN 3: Yeah. The English Rose. She's walking.

DONA: That's a lie.

CITIZEN 4: You'd have seen her for yourself only she got the Forrest Gump. She just ran and ran. God knows where she is.

OMO: Now do you believe?

ALL: I believe. Help me!

The CITIZENS crowd around OMO begging him for help.

DONA: That's a lie! He's insane. He's been in the madhouse. He thought he was the Prime Minister. He's suffering another episode. He's a mad foundling looking for his daddy. It's true. Ask him.

CITIZENS freeze.

OMO looks at DONA and at the CITIZENS. He walks away, leaving them behind.

I knew you wouldn't fall for his falsehood. You're Brixtonians. You've seen and heard it all /

CITIZENS: (*As they run after OMO.*) Omo, please help me, help me! (*They exit after OMO.*)

DONA turns ferociously to GREG. GREG cowers, thinking she's going to slap him again.

DONA: Help me stop this madness. We can expose him.

GREG: So you really aren't part of his scheme.

DONA: I can't let The Mission find out about this.

GREG: You're on your own, 'sister'. (*Brings out his mobile phone.*) Hi, this is... (*DONA is still there.*) Hold on... Don't you have a saviour to crucify?

75

DONA, exasperated, exits.

(*On the phone. During the conversation he changes into JASON.
He puts on black gloves and dark glasses.*) Jason, it's Greg. Greg
from… Yes, that Greg. I've got something for you. Yes he's
a threat to national security. No he's not got a beard. No
he doesn't have a rucksack. Listen to me! This is bigger
than anything you've seen. I'm talking Roundheads and
Chartists. Yes, the R-word. I want guarantees first. It's not
what you can offer me. It's what I want. Yes, take your
bloody time…

GREG is now JASON.

JASON: (*Covers the phone.*) Now I remember Greg. Ambitious
bastard. So the natives in SW4 are being woken up from
their slumber. Should be a police matter but when the
rabble congregates and revolution is mentioned, it's my
job to see to things. That recessive Norman gene pops up
in unexpected places. I won't let them storm the Palace.
Greg could be exaggerating but if he's not it's my head on
the block. I'll promise him whatever for his information
and after that he can go fuck himself. I'm not that high up
the ladder yet. And this Omo character seems just the one
to fast track me to the penthouse suite of policy making.
(*To GREG.*) Greg? Yes. You will be getting a call from the
Secretary after we nullify this threat. Now give me the
details. (*Covers the phone. To the audience, menacingly.*) Excuse
me. For my ears only.

*MARIA in the gentleman's club. It is empty. She is bewildered.
She takes off her coat and wraps herself around the pole. She
dances half-heartedly and stops. SARAH enters, running. She
jogs on the spot, facing the audience. MARIA, who does not notice
her, takes a bottle of pills from her bag. She swallows the lot.
She crumbles to the floor. Finally she loses consciousness. As she
loses consciousness, SARAH slows down until she stops. She covers
MARIA with the Union Jack and exits.*

Brixton High Street.

CITIZENS running in different directions calling out OMO's name.
They run off in different directions, leaving behind CITIZENS 1
and 2.

CITIZEN 1: (*Huffs.*) You sure he's not in the Barrier Block?

CITIZEN 2: (*Testily.*) We're both coming from there, aren't we?

CITIZEN 1: Man, I got to catch my breath. (*Sits down.*)

CITIZEN 2: He'll be out of miracles by the time we find him.

CITIZEN 1: I'm not Sarah Green, I can't keep running all over
Brixton. What's the rush? He's the real deal. He's here to
stay.

CITIZEN 2: So was Windows 95.

CITIZEN 1: Give me a few minutes.

CITIZEN 2 reluctantly sits down.

You thought I was stupid jumping from one faith to
another.

CITIZEN 2: You have to admit: saying 'Allah Akbar' in a
synagogue had you pinned down as the classic confused
black man. Where's your beads?

CITIZEN 1: (*Looks down at his chest.*) Ha! They must have come
off when we was all running after Omo. When I see him
I'm asking for a B-Mer covered in beads. And he has to
bring Bob Marley back to life. I worship the nits in his
locks.

CITIZEN 2: He might be in the Juice Bar. (*Stands up.*) Come on.
It's only up the road. (*Holds out his hand. Pulls up CITIZEN 1.*)

CITIZEN 1: (*Exclaims with tiredness.*) So now you've seen what
he can do, what are you going to ask him for? And please
don't say world peace.

CITIZEN 2: (*Thinks.*) I don't know.

They exit.

ROBBIE is sleeping on a bench. He is enjoying the sweetest dream. OMO enters, with a stick. He takes off his caftan and proceeds to flagellate himself.

ROBBIE: (*In his sleep.*) Yes Baby, I've been a naughty boy... (*He stirs. Sees OMO.*) Hey! (*Takes the stick away from OMO. Inspects OMO's back.*) Reasonable chastisement, that's what the law states, yeah.

OMO: What's the time?

ROBBIE: I don't know. The town hall clock stopped working since that stunt you pulled with Sarah.

OMO: You don't believe that I /

ROBBIE: I've lived in Brixton all my life. I take everything I see with a pinch of salt.

OMO: But you saw it.

ROBBIE: I dunno, I mean, I saw her running yeah but... So you did make her... Wow. That is some serious shit!

OMO: I made a mistake.

ROBBIE: Man, I'd like to make mistakes like that. So you're really /

OMO: I thought Maria was the sign.

ROBBIE: Don't beat yourself up about it. I still can't believe it.

OMO: I am not worthy. I cannot lead the overthrow of the wilful peace.

ROBBIE: Man I thought you was some joker. So you gonna build that bomb? (*Sits down next to OMO.*)

OMO: No.

ROBBIE: This is your chance. You've got the whole of Brixton on your side. People don't care about you being loopy.

OMO: But they are in so deep. They do not recognise their collaboration in their own oppression.

ROBBIE: You still don't get it. This is a country with a history of failed revolutions, of reforms passed off as radical change. Co-optation has been the order from day one. The people, your people, they realised that ages ago. They're like the unions. They've become an interest group holding out for a bigger cut of the capitalist pie.

OMO: I should have waited for the call.

ROBBIE: Surely you should know Eve was the downfall of Adam. Why else do you think Woman stands for Woe Onto Man?

OMO: It is not Maria's fault.

ROBBIE: You should know me by now. Me and women, we're like oil and water. I'm not a shoulder you can cry on either. You fuck up, you fuck up. Take it on the chin and move on.

OMO: The bell has stopped ringing.

ROBBIE: That Mission girl said some nasty stuff about you. This isn't about you wanting a family you never had, is it?

OMO: Is that too much to want?

ROBBIE: When you're trying to lead a revolution, yes.

OMO: I want Brixton as my family. I want the world as my family. And that can only come with peace, Robbie. It can only come when no man is subservient to another. I don't want to be alone anymore in the world. It's not right. We must love one another, Robbie, or the cycle of pain will continue.

ROBBIE: Bruv, pain's part of being human. Deal with it.

OMO: Pain is all I've dealt with. I never knew my parents. When you're told you were dumped in a bin... I got adopted by a Nigerian couple. They'd lost three children, one after the other. They believed that it was a spirit child always coming and going between here and the spirit world. The pastor of their Celestial Church told them that I was their spirit child returned. They gave me the bangles and this to prevent me from dying. (*Reveals the rock pendant.*) I also got this (*Shows him the cross scar.*) so that if I did die again and I returned they'd know it was me.

ROBBIE: So, are you like a reincarnation?

OMO: I survived. Since then I've always thought I was special, the chosen one, and everything I did pointed towards doing something great in my life. I took off my shirt during PE, the teacher saw the scar. She called social services and I got taken off them. Until I became a man I was being pushed from one home to the other. I have been a wanderer. The only place I felt I belonged to was here. Here where I was left to die.

ROBBIE: So you're normal.

OMO: Once in a while I feel a force tugging at me, trying to pull me out of this world. I don't know. I do know that I love Maria and I love this world.

ROBBIE: It's not me you want to shag. Tell Maria. I'm sure she'll believe you.

OMO: And what do I tell the people of Brixton?

ROBBIE: Hey, I'm already walking a tightrope with advice on how to bag totty.

OMO: Please.

ROBBIE: You really want my opinion?

OMO: For all it's worth.

ROBBIE: For all it's worth. Next time, tell the people that you are the Christ of the End Times. And that the fire and brimstone arrives on time tomorrow. That will put a rocket up their arses.

OMO: Fire and brimstone. That is so old school.

ROBBIE: It works. You haven't been clipped round the ear by my Aunt Petunia.

OMO: If I convince Brixtonians that the time has come, will you join me in building the New Jerusalem?

ROBBIE: Sure. Giro doesn't go that far in this world anyway.

OMO: You will be my rock. When the bell rings again, you will know it is time.

ROBBIE: Obviously you know nothing about council maintenance. Clear off. Now! Your peeps are waiting and man needs to dream. (*Lies down.*)

OMO leaves.

Omo!

OMO turns round.

You got a pound?

They smile.

CITIZENS OF BRIXTON rush round looking for OMO. They set up the gentleman's club and continue to look for OMO. They exit.

SARAH runs in and jogs on the spot, centre-stage.

SARAH: You know what it feels like when you're serving a higher purpose. My legs are my wings. This is worth more than a medal. This is worth more than being on the back of a cereal pack. I will run round Brixton and this time the people will follow me. We shall march across the river and the walls of the city shall fall. I haven't heard the bell ring yet: I'm still waiting for the word. The people are still scratching around, looking for their own little patch of Albion. Soon their ears will open and the scales will fall from their eyes. They will see the New Jerusalem on the horizon and raise a mighty shout! For Brixton! For England! For Britain!

SARAH runs out.

The gentleman's club. MARIA, sitting up, covered in the Union Jack as before. OMO stands beside her.

MARIA: So why didn't you tell me all this before?

OMO: I tried to but first I wanted you to believe in me. Are you sure you're all right?

MARIA: I slipped and fell. I'm fine.

OMO: Covered in the flag.

MARIA: I was doing my dervish number.

OMO: Soon the past will die and tomorrow will herald a new beginning.

MARIA: I know what I am in this world. In this life.

OMO: And I know who you are in the New World.

MARIA looks away.

Don't be afraid of the future, of the storm before the calm.

MARIA: What if the storm never blows over?

OMO: Maria…

MARIA: Let someone else be the Christ of Coldharbour Lane.

OMO: The what?

MARIA: Please. I don't like where this is leading.

OMO: You have called me by my name. Say you believe in me. Say it, Maria, say it.

MARIA: You made a cripple to walk. What do you need me for?

OMO: When the world goes to sleep I don't want to be alone.

MARIA: And if you decide to become someone else and leave me, what do I do then?

OMO: I will never leave you. Now say it.

A CITIZEN enters.

CITIZEN: I knew I'd find you here. Saturday's lottery numbers and I promise I won't tell a soul. You and your woman can make nookie in peace. Hey, Maria, I wet myself because of you… (*Wets himself.*) Oh-oh.

OMO: I will return soon.

CITIZEN: (*As they exit.*) Brother Omo, can you spare a brother one of your handkerchiefs? My, er, river's burst its banks again. (*He bumps into a chair.*) Sorry, I must be going blind.

OMO exits with CITIZEN.

MARIA brings out the bottle of tablets from where it is hidden inside the flag. She weeps.

JASON enters. She does not notice him. He knocks the bottle from her hands.

MARIA: Who are you?

JASON: Where can I find Omo?

MARIA: What do you want him for?

JASON: Where is he?

MARIA: I don't know.

JASON: Where is Omo?

MARIA: I don't know!

JASON closes in on her.

(*Backs away.*) I said I don't know, I don't know, I don't know…

OMO and CITIZEN. CITIZEN has a lottery ticket and a pen at the ready.

CITIZEN: Ones haven't come up at all this month. You think it might come up this Saturday?

OMO holds CITIZEN's hand.

Or maybe not. You know I can go with all what you said before about the wilful peace. But not just yet. Guys aren't ready for that. You got to find the right time to lay down the heavy stuff. Ease us in.

OMO: The right time… (*Feels a tug. The sound of singing and praying.*)

CITIZEN: Omo, are you OK?

OMO sways as he is caught between two worlds. He fights to stay in this world. The sound of Yoruba Christian singing punctuated by a baby laughing joyously.

OMO: I say to you always it is time to shake off your chains. Always it is time to destroy the wilful peace. A new world beckons. The New Jerusalem will rise in Britain and Brixton shall be the citadel.

DONA, by the station. She is praying. She has a bell. No one is listening to her.

DONA: What a time to suffer a crisis of faith. What am I supposed to do? I've heard from the elders. They've withheld my promotion subject to an inquiry. I had my collar in the bag. But now I don't know if I've been running around for The Mission for the wrong reasons. I have done some good in my life. I am not a bad person. I've done everything that was required to make me a better person. I got this bell. I thought, if I'd ring it I'd put the genie back into his bottle. He'd stop hearing Alfie and this would turn out to be a bad dream. But now I'm too afraid to ring it. What do I do now? Tell me, what am I supposed to do in a situation like this? Show me a sign. Please.

SARAH runs by. DONA sees her. She is shaken by the sight of her running.

Sister Sarah! Sarah!

SARAH stops.

You know you can never compete again. They'll test you for every drug under the sun. You will test positive for every one of them.

SARAH: Don't be afraid, Dona.

DONA: (*Takes a step back.*) I'm not afraid.

SARAH: Then ask. (*Holds DONA.*) It's all right. Everything will be all right. Believe. That's all you have to do. The people will truly believe and they will come out for the crossing of the river. (*She takes DONA's bell and runs off.*) They will come out and we will shake the city to its foundation! Say the word! Say the word!

JASON enters running. He stops in front of DONA.

JASON: That was Sarah Green?

DONA: Yes.

JASON makes to run after SARAH. He turns round. He looks into his PDA and recognises DONA.

JASON: Dona?

DONA: Yes? And you are?

JASON: Where is Omo?

DONA: He's no longer with The Mission.

JASON: That wasn't my question.

DONA: That's the answer you're going to get.

JASON approaches DONA menacingly. SARAH runs across ringing the bell.

SARAH: Come out for the crossing of the river! Shake off the wilful peace! (*She stands on one side of the stage.*) The word is coming!

JASON runs after her.

The gentleman's club, on one half of the stage. Brixton High Street on the other half where the scene between JASON and SARAH takes place simultaneously.

MARIA is lying on the floor unconscious. Her face is bloodied.

OMO enters.

OMO: Maria... Maria! (*He cradles her in his arms.*) Maria, talk to me. Maria! (*He takes off his rock pendant and the ankle bracelet. He puts them on MARIA. He drops two handkerchiefs over her.*)

Music.

Blessed mother. You are bridging the gap between worlds. You are causing joy to reign in the kingdoms. The seed on earth has been planted. There will be no more painful returns, no more fruitless journeys. Your journey is not at an end. Here in Brixton where the new foundation will be built. Stand up and dance. I have ignited the rhythm to drive your passion for life. Get up and dance a new dance! Dance for joy. Dance for life.

Slowly, MARIA rises. She picks up the handkerchiefs and dances. It is not the dance of the gentleman's club but one of joy and happiness. She kisses OMO's feet.

These are the last tears you will weep – Mother.

The sound of a heartbeat. MARIA touches her stomach. She stands up. They kiss. She dances. Blinding light bathes them both.

SARAH runs by. JASON runs after her with a hammer. He stops to catch his breath.

SARAH runs past him. He stops her. They argue. He drags her offstage.

JASON enters. His hands are bloody.

JASON: You are witnesses. You saw me try to reason with her. She didn't want her old life back. No, no more for her the glory of the podium. She'd rather be the poster child for Omo's New Jerusalem. What a fool. I just hope she hasn't

woken up the natives with that bloody bell. (*Looks around.*)
I guess not. They didn't wake up when she got healed, did
they? The clueless sods. They're not like us. I'll protect you
from them and halt this idiotic revolution. The state will
reward me with a seat in their inner circle. That's all you
can ask for out of life. I know it and you know it so shut
your mouths and get with the programme.

MARIA dances offstage. JASON walks across to OMO.

OMO: (*With great relief.*) I knew it. My time has come. Our
time has come. Sarah, you can now gather the crowds.
I know what to tell them. Their ears will open and we
shall tear down the city brick by brick. We shall rip every
banknote to pieces. We shall melt every coin. We shall
burn every deed, every leasehold. We shall dig up every
gate in our path. We shall reclaim the land! There will be
an outpouring of freedom the likes of which this nation has
never seen.

JASON: You couldn't convince them with your watered down
tosh, how are you going to convince them with this?

OMO: The timing. Alfie will ring his bell. And all who have
ears will hear. All who have eyes will see.

JASON: You're waiting to hear the bells of a dead man /

OMO: Sh!

*Faintly, in the distance the sound of a bell. It sounds different
from the town hall bell.*

OMO: You hear it? Ring, Alfie, ring!

JASON: This game is over. (*Brings out a knife.*)

OMO: No, it has only just begun. My Father has said it: I will
not die. Lastborns get it…

*JASON stabs him. OMO smiles curiously at him. His hands reveal
blood. JASON stabs him again and again. OMO dies. JASON looks
around for somewhere to hide him. He picks up the flag. As he*

is about to cover OMO's body, he realises he's picked up the flag. He puts it down and drags his body offstage.

Sound of the bell getting louder.

SARAH's flat, signified by a medal.

DONA, MARIA, cleaning up SARAH.

DONA: I swear I found her like this.

MARIA: Why didn't you take her to a hospital?

DONA: I tried. She didn't want to go.

MARIA: Sarah, say something. Sarah, where is Omo?

DONA: I thought he was with you.

MARIA: He was, then I started dancing. And then I came across you.

DONA: Come on, Sarah, please. Who did this to you?

MARIA: Like you don't know.

DONA: How could you think such a thing! I wouldn't hurt Sarah. I wouldn't hurt Omo either.

MARIA: Oh my God. That man. He did it!

DONA: Who? Which man?

MARIA: There was a man asking for Omo. He tried to kill me.

DONA: But there's not even a cut on you.

Pause. MARIA takes in this knowledge.

MARIA: I've got to find Omo.

DONA: Be careful. I think I might have bumped into him. He looks like bad news.

SARAH moans. The bell gets louder. The sound of people gathering.

Do you hear that? It's Omo!

MARIA: Stay here. Sarah can't go out in her condition.

SARAH moans angrily.

DONA: But she wants to go.

MARIA: And give you a chance to prove that Omo is a lie?

DONA: Believe me, Maria, this is way beyond that. The people will find out sooner or later about Sarah. We have to find that man before he gets to Omo.

MARIA: I'll be back soon.

MARIA exits into a sound of people gathering. DONA and SARAH withdraw.

CITIZEN 1: I heard a bell.

CITIZEN 2: I heard it too.

CITIZEN 1: The bell led us all here.

CITIZEN 2: It had a familiar ring to it. Sounded very much like Alfie's bell.

CITIZEN 1: No it didn't.

CITIZEN 2: Yes it did.

CITIZEN 1: Doesn't mean it's Alfie's bell. It could have been Sarah ringing a bell for all I know.

CITIZEN 2: Where is Sarah?

CITIZEN 1: Could be she's gone out of Brixton. Could have been the town hall clock ringing. (*Looks up at the clock.*) No?

CITIZEN 2: It's still out of order.

CITIZEN 1: Who cares who's ringing what bell anyway? Where's Omo?

CITIZENS: (*Chant.*) Where is Omo? Where is Omo?

MARIA enters stricken with a bloody handkerchief.

*JASON enters from the other side of the stage. He is startled on
seeing MARIA. His startled look turns into a smile when he sees
the bloody handkerchief.*

CITIZEN 1: It's Maria! Where's Omo?

MARIA: I don't know where he is.

CITIZEN 2: What do you mean you don't know? What's that?

MARIA: You cannot be afraid now. You cannot turn back. The
seed has been planted. If there was ever a sign to cross the
river this is it! This is it. Get your handkerchiefs and wave
them. Wave them like you've never done before and let's
go!

CITIZEN 1: I ain't following you! What's happened to Omo?

MARIA: It was never about Omo. It's about you. It's about
all of us and the things we can do if we believe that the
impossible is always possible. So come on, wave your
handkerchiefs!

CITIZEN 2: I'm waving nothing until you tell us what's
happened to him.

JASON laughs.

MARIA: All he's been asking is for you to begin the journey
in your hearts. Right here, right now. Can you do that?
Because it doesn't matter if he's here or not. He's been
here with you and what did you ask for? So come on! Let's
go.

CITIZEN 2: We'll follow you. For now.

They do not wave their handkerchiefs.

*JASON moves forward menacingly. DONA wheels in SARAH. JASON
stops. He claps.*

Uproar of shocked CITIZENS.

CITIZEN 1: What the hell is this?

CITIZEN 2: Oh my God, it's Sarah!

MARIA: Why? Dona, why?

DONA: She wanted to come. I couldn't take her wailing. I'm sorry, Maria.

MARIA: It is ended.

SARAH raises her handkerchief. She waves it furiously as she rocks back and forth. The bell rings louder.

SARAH: (*Struggles with her speech.*) Shake off the wilful peace! Shake off the wilful peace!

CITIZENS: (*Slowly they begin to wave their handkerchiefs.*) Shake off the wilful peace.

White handkerchiefs flutter and cover the stage.

JASON brings out his mobile phone.

SARAH beckons to DONA to push her. JASON blocks their path.

JASON: It's over!

SARAH points at JASON.

End this charade now before I do. (*Threatens to use his mobile.*)

OMO walks across the stage, unseen but felt. He exits. The town hall bell rings.

MARIA: Across the river! To London Bridge!

DONA: To where?

MARIA: To the City! To the City!

JASON is knocked to the ground. He is trampled to death.

Blackout.

Soundscape: marching turns to rioting. Gunshots.

Windrush Square. A year later. Winter. Snow covers the ground.

ROBBIE: We haven't gained so much to lose it all by being careless, you get me? So I'm saying this for the last time. Check with our doctors before you take any medicine. Okay? Infiltrators, traitors, it's all in the game. The enemy will throw whatever they've got at us. One year is a drop in the ocean of history. We've done so well to come this far. And are we backing down?

CITIZENS: No!

SARAH is wheeled in by DONA.

ROBBIE: So keep on being your brother's keeper. Keep looking out for one another. The journey is long but we knew that when we set foot on the road. There ain't no miracles in this world.

CITIZEN 1: I'd still like a bit of KFC every now and again though.

ROBBIE: So long as Colonel Sanders isn't leading our troops.

CITIZEN 2: When's the heating coming back on?

ROBBIE: Our engineers are working on it. The heating, the electricity, the water. We might have lost Battersea but we took enough equipment from the old power station. The Tulse Hill power station will soon be online. Don't you worry about it, all right? This is us saying and doing. This is us staking our claim. And aren't you proud?

CITIZENS: Yeah!

ROBBIE: I thought I heard you say that.

DONA: Say it, Robbie!

SARAH: (*Cheers.*)

ROBBIE continues addressing the crowd in silence.

DONA: It's almost three.

SARAH: (*Shakes her head.*)

DONA: Okay, we'll stay but only for a little while longer. The therapist will go mad if you're late again.

MARIA enters, pushing a pram. She has a gun.

DONA: Hi, Maria.

MARIA: Hi Dona, hi Sarah.

DONA: How's junior?

MARIA: As sweet as ever.

DONA: Oh, that birthmark's getting uglier by the day. What did the GP say?

SARAH gestures to MARIA. MARIA takes the baby out and hands him to SARAH.

MARIA: I haven't been.

DONA: Maria!

MARIA: It's fine. I know what it is.

DONA: And what did I tell you about the bracelet?

MARIA: Just making sure he's not going anywhere.

DONA: He can't crawl yet.

MARIA: It's for my own peace of mind. Do you miss The Mission?

DONA: Not as much as I thought.

MARIA: You heard about the clinic they set up in West Norwood?

DONA: Yes. You can't change people overnight.

MARIA: Yeah but you can't ask people to convert while they're vulnerable. They'll say anything to get treated.

DONA: They do have good people working for them.

MARIA: So you do miss being with them.

DONA: We've all got to move on.

CITIZENS: (*Shout.*) Complacency!

ROBBIE: So let me ask you once again. What will send our society back to square one?

CITIZENS: Complacency!

ROBBIE: I thought I heard you say that.

DONA: Robbie's on form today.

MARIA: Is he ever.

CITIZEN 2: Is it true the Manchester crew have captured Cheshire?

ROBBIE: Where have you been, bruv? Our friends in the North aren't the only ones making gains. Liverpool, Newcastle, Leeds, Nottingham, Birmingham and Glasgow, our units have all made gains. We've made up for losses in Stoke and Edinburgh.

CITIZEN 1: I hear we took a beating in Llanelli.

ROBBIE: We're getting more Welsh speakers to translate the road signs. You live and you learn.

MARIA: Amazing how those men we let out of Brixton prison were so willing to join the fight.

DONA: I know. I thought they were going to run off or cause havoc. It's like they had been preparing for this moment all their lives.

MARIA: Just when we thought the battle was lost. Talk about turning the tide.

ROBBIE: Big up to Commander Maudlin, just returned from leading A section to reclaim Elephant and Castle.

CITIZENS cheer.

ROBBIE: Now she's off to help D section hold Waterloo Bridge. I salute your indefatigable spirit.

CITIZENS cheer.

DONA: You be careful.

MARIA: I will. (*To the baby.*) Won't we, Babatunde?

A bell rings.

The End.

www.ingramcontent.com/pod-product-compliance
Ingram Content Group UK Ltd.
Pitfield, Milton Keynes, MK11 3LW, UK
UKHW020724280225
455688UK00012B/497